everything I'm not made me everything I am

Everything I'm Not Made Me Everything I Am

DISCOVERING YOUR PERSONAL BEST

JEFF JOHNSON

SMILEYBOOKS

Distributed by Hay House, Inc.

Carlsbad, California • New York City
London • Sydney • Johannesburg
Vancouver • Hong Kong • New Delhi

Published in the United States by: SmileyBooks, 250 Park Avenue South, Suite #201, New York, NY 10003

Distributed in the United States by: Hay House, Inc.: www.hayhouse.com • ***Published and distributed in Australia by:*** Hay House Australia Pty. Ltd.: www.hayhouse.com.au • ***Published and distributed in the United Kingdom by:*** Hay House UK, Ltd.: www.hayhouse.co.uk • ***Published and distributed in the Republic of South Africa by:*** Hay House SA (Pty), Ltd.: www.hayhouse.co.za • ***Distributed in Canada by:*** Raincoast: www.raincoast.com • ***Published and distributed in India by:*** Hay House Publishers India: www.hayhouse.com

Design: Jen Kennedy

Library of Congress Cataloging-in-Publication Data

Johnson, Jeff (Jeffrey I.).
Everything I'm not made me everything I am : discovering your pesonal best / Jeff Johnson. -- 1st ed.
p. cm.
ISBN 978-1-4019-2548-2
1. Self-realization. 2. Success. 3. Achievement motivation. I. Title.
BF637.S4J637 2009
158.1--dc22

2009019650

ISBN: 978-1-4019-2548-2

12 11 10 09 4 3 2 1
1st edition, September 2009

Printed in the United States of America

To **Mom and Dad**
for being my models and
Madison, Myles, and **Malcolm**
for being my inspiration.

I love you.

• • •

Foreword xi
Introduction xiii

PART I: Blow Up to Break Through

Chapter 1. Breaking Out of Jail 3
Chapter 2. I Am Not My Parents 13
Chapter 3. I Am Whole 31

PART II: Envision, Experiment, and Engineer

Chapter 4. Can You See It? 47
Chapter 5. The Jump-Off Point 55
Chapter 6. Build Your Team 67
Chapter 7. Give All of Yourself 83

PART III: Strategize, Streamline, and Sacrifice

Chapter 8. Strategize: Plan for Your Best 99
Chapter 9. Transform Mistakes into Opportunity 117
Chapter 10. Conquer Conflict Crossroads 133
Chapter 11. Solitude: Learn to Stand Alone 147

PART IV: Living Your Best

Chapter 12. Confirmation 165
Chapter 13. Fulfillment 173

Acknowledgments 181
About the Author 183

FOREWORD

When Jeff first came to me about this book, I had to step back for a second and remember what I was thinking when I wrote "Everything I Am." It's crazy, because so many people think they know who we are. They see us at the job or on the street and make assumptions about what we're like. They swear they know our story, what we've been through, and who we're supposed to be. But they don't know the half of it. Most of the time we're trying to figure it out ourselves.

Because I've dedicated my life to the pursuit of my purpose, I'm not quick to hype someone I don't believe is for real. Jeff Johnson is for real. I remember the first time I met Jeff. He and I were on the same panel for one of Russell Simmons's Hip-Hop Summits back in 2004. When I heard him speak—and more than that, when we had a chance to build with him—I thought this guy is an asset to our community.

This book will teach you your best differently than any other book out there. Jeff first makes you deal with those hard questions that you sometimes don't want to deal with. Attacking all the issues that have been keeping you from being your best has to happen if you ever want to make your life what it was created to be. Everything I'm Not goes deeper than just telling you how to get paid. It breaks down how to be your "real self." As somebody who's won the plaques, the awards, and made the money, I can tell you that there is more to life than these things. Don't get me wrong, they're good—they're actually great—but they're not everything. I know a lot of people who are getting paid, but are empty on the inside. This book is an A to Z on how to be fulfilled.

I recommend you read it cover to cover and share it with your friends and family. Jeff's words and thoughts are real in a world filled with fakers. Everything I'm Not is guaranteed to inspire, empower, and help everyone young and not so young to be his or her BEST. Before you even start to read it, I'm challenging you to do more than flip the pages. When you're done reading, answer the hard questions and then do the hard part . . . Be YOU.

— **Kanye West**
May 2009

INTRODUCTION

"Stop the bullshit!"

Harsh, I know. The words cut even now when I think about them. Not just the first or second, but the countless times in my past that I looked in the mirror blurting the obscenity and saw someone looking back who was falling short of who he was capable of becoming. Was the statement totally true? No. However, it was a reflection of how I felt about my level of effort, and thus the reality of certain aspects of my life. So the harsh self-evaluation was necessary for me to walk away from that mirror and attempt to create a new reality based on becoming my best and stop living in a state of mediocrity.

For nearly a decade, I've seen people who've been standing in front of the same mirror. I've traveled around the world speaking with professionals, young adults, and college students about everything from policy and political activism to popular culture and purpose. I've lectured at Ivy League institutions and have conducted workshops at historically black colleges. I've also counseled professionals in industries ranging from journalism to advertising, and consulted with elected officials at the local, state, and national levels. Through these experiences, I've met some of the best and brightest people who are working to change the world for the better. However, during question and answer sessions, side conversations, post-event correspondence, and consulting sessions, it becomes obvious that these brilliant people are in front of the same mirror challenging themselves to be better. So, while they may not be beating themselves up or cursing themselves out, they're looking for something more than their great opportunities, jobs, money, success, or even fame can give them—the fulfillment that comes from living one's personal best.

I find it interesting that many companies, colleges, and training centers around the world are helping people develop skills and secure positions, titles, and money, but they're not guiding them through a process of actually becoming their personal best. I've seen the 4.0 college student who's lost, and the multimillionaire entrepreneur who's empty. They exist in this space of dissatisfaction because becoming your personal best is not simply about achieving success in one area of your life, but creating a model of living that propels you to excel in every aspect of your life. I want to see that 4.0 student also happy about his personal relationships, and poised to take an internship that will translate into a career he loves. I want to see that unfulfilled entrepreneur training others how to do what she did, making a global contribution by traveling the world, experiencing new cultures and operating in a complete model of excellence. I want to see each of us claim our limitless potential by living whole and fulfilled lives.

I recognized in my own life that until I stepped away from the mirror and strived to be my best self every day, I was going to continue to stand at that mirror frustrated and dissatisfied. I am continuing to walk a life's journey that has helped me discover and fight for the best that's within me in all aspects of my life. I want you to be able to do the same. In this book, I'll take you through a process that will challenge you to blow up old notions of who you are not, so that you can become who you're supposed to be.

I wrote this book because you need it. Don't get me wrong. You don't need me. However, you do need a process that goes beyond getting paid, because some of you have money. You need a process—some real, tangible, best practices—that extend farther than showing you how to find a mate or have kids, because many of you have a spouse, significant other, or even a boo. You need a road map that shows you how to travel beyond success in one isolated aspect of your life, because many of you are well on your way and others have already become successful in this or that. What you need, and what I've designed this book to provide, is help to guide you on your journey to a place of fulfillment.

Think of me as your guide on this journey. Like many of you, I've gained a measure of success in certain areas of my life. My professional career has been amazing, and I wake up every day loving the work that I do. I have been an All-American athlete, a youth pastor, a leadership trainer, an international journalist, and a business owner.

However, I realized in gaining that success that I'd started to ignore significant parts of my life that make me who I am. As a result, I had terrible personal relationships and a failed marriage, and I spent far too much time away from my kids. I was successful, yet fragmented, and thus a mediocre man. I knew I had to create a process that would challenge my weaknesses and push me to become a great man and not just a "successful professional." Am I great yet? No! But I'm committed to working every day to get there. It is that trip—my journey of failure transformed to focus and my mediocrity transformed to mastery—that I'll use to guide you through the process to become your personal best.

This book is based on a combination of life experiences learned in the trenches and invaluable lessons taught to me by mentors. These lessons have given me insights that have helped—by default and on purpose—to create a set of best practices that have guided me to achieving my personal best.

What exactly is a best practice? It's a technique or methodology, gained through experience and research, that's been proven to reliably and consistently lead to a desired result. In other words, best practices assemble the most essential ingredients and processes required to produce outstanding results. We can learn a great deal by observing why and how other people have done their best to become their best. By learning how to identify and apply best practices, I'm living a life that years ago I thought was absolutely impossible. And I know that, by continuing to follow this path toward my personal best, my next decade will be even better.

I want to introduce you to a path and the processes that will:

- Break you out of the maze of mediocrity
- Challenge you to discover who you are not
- Help you create a defining vision
- Show you how to find your jump-off point
- Build your terrific team
- Teach you to give your best to get your best
- Transform your mistakes into positive manifestations
- Conquer your Conflict Crossroads
- Unleash your power to stand alone
- Appreciate your life's confirmations
- Celebrate your personal best

Everything I'm Not Made Me Everything I Am is not about you getting paid, or famous, or hired. It is about getting YOU to that place known as your personal best. It's that space in your life where you bring together the professional, the personal, and even the spiritual, and create a lifestyle in which you expect and accept nothing less than excellence every day. Your personal best will not allow you to be a successful businessperson but a terrible father, or be a super mom who neglects her passion to become a professor. Becoming your personal best is about more than simply how others feel about what you do. It is equally about how you feel about who you are. I ask you to commit to the process with all you have. You cannot give half of yourself to this journey and succeed.

I'm not offering you a model that gets you more stuff. Reading this book will not help you find a mate in seven days, fix your credit score in four weeks, or get you rich in ten steps. It's not a journey to wealth or fame. It demonstrates a process that can help you discover and rediscover invaluable best practices that can support your desire to live your personal best: what it looks like, how to get to it and, most important, how to maintain it . . .

I know it sounds corny, but achieving your personal best is a feeling—an unshakable sense that the inner and outer you actually match. Your life has meaning because you've gained mastery of yourself. I guarantee you that the feeling of living a fulfilling life beats gaining the material trappings of a capitalist society any day. For my die-hard capitalist friends out there: a fulfilling life positions you to maximize your gifts in a way a mediocre and fragmented existence never can, no matter how big your bling. Your personal best is the gateway to money, power, respect, love, and positions that don't sacrifice who you really are to gain them. When you place getting "stuff" before gaining fulfillment, you find yourself in the rat race for someone else. And when that happens, you may be forced to realize that this lifetime is and always has been about you. This book asks that you learn how to live from your depth and not your surface, so that you can give the world your best.

Are you ready to take this journey? Take a moment and really look at your reflection in the mirror and ask yourself: Are you ready to become all that you were meant to be? Now's the time—the time for you to challenge the only person who has not only the power to stand in your way, but also, more important, the power to transform you from pedestrian to phenomenal. YOU! Are you ready to break the mirror of mediocrity and reflect the brilliance of your personal best? If you're ready, I'm ready. Let's go!

PART I

BLOW UP TO BREAK THROUGH

CHAPTER 1

Breaking Out of Jail

I can't promise you that the journey toward your personal best is going to be an easy one because few major accomplishments ever are. However, I can promise you that it'll be worth every step.

A few months ago, my six-year-old son and I were watching one of the older Las Vegas casinos being demolished on TV. As the decades-old building imploded on itself, the dust of years past rose into the dark night air even as the walls themselves tumbled to the ground, and I was struck by how efficiently the demolition experts had razed the building in less than a minute.

My son, however, had a very different reaction as the monstrous structure came falling to the ground. He asked, "Why did they blow it up? Why couldn't they just knock it down?"

I explained to him that knocking the building down would just take a large structure and spread it out into smaller chunks. This way, blowing the building up made it easier to clean up and build anew. Even as I spoke these words aloud to my son, I realized that, too often, we're just knocking stuff over in our own lives, believing we've solved the problem, when we have actually just spread it out and made it harder for ourselves to clean up and start over.

Just as progress demanded the casino blow up to make room for new opportunity, our lives sometimes demand that we, too, blow up old thinking, old ways of behaving, and a false identity that stand in the way of our moving to the next level. These distortions are the prisons that create a false self and they must be destroyed if we're to move beyond our limitations. This isn't always easy to do. Too often, it's not other people, places, or things that hold us back, but our very selves, our false selves.

To blow up your false self—the mediocre self—you have to be willing to break through to your new self—the best self. If we can truly allow ourselves to consider demolishing our old fears and doubts, beginning anew with a fresh foundation of promise and hope, we can literally create new lives for ourselves, regardless of our pasts. You can begin by examining your false self because, in my experience, the biggest thing holding you back from your personal best is a false sense of who you are.

Jiwe's Story

As I began writing this chapter about blowing up false identities and breaking through to who you really are, I signed up to become the spokesperson for a movement called Healing Starts With Us. This movement was inspired by *Black Pain: It Just Looks Like We're Not Hurting*, written by PR expert and author Terrie Williams. The book focuses on the depression that plagues the African American community, a depression that too often goes unaddressed and, as a result, unhealed. Unexpressed pain is one of the deep reservoirs of that which contributes to false notions of yourself—all the things you are not. These are the obstacles that have to be blown up so that you can break through to who you really are.

During a press conference for the Healing Starts With Us campaign, I met a young man named Dashaun "Jiwe" Morris. Jiwe's book, *War of the Bloods in My Veins: A Street Soldier's March Toward Redemption*, describes how he lost his first friend in a drive-by shooting in the fourth grade, and how Jiwe himself gives in to the violence of his neighborhood. He becomes a drug dealer, a carjacker, and a member of the Bloods street gang—until one night, he almost shoots a close friend who was hanging out with young men he thought were members of his rival gang, the Crips.

What captured me about this story was how it connected to this very idea of blowing up to break through. Jiwe's story was not the stereotypical story of a brother behind bars who becomes enlightened because of incarceration. No, Jiwe's story is not as simple, or as straightforward, as that. Jiwe discovered who he was by realizing who he was not. He realized that being a part of this violent street gang was not who he really was or what was meant for him. This was not his destiny, even though Jiwe's father had been one of the original architects of the Bloods in the sixties. Being in the Bloods was in Jiwe's blood.

Jiwe recognized the standoff taking place in his soul between the man people said he was and the man he was destined to become if he dared to change his life. He recognized that he was so much more than the issues and the violence that surrounded him in the community where he grew up. It was then that he made a revolutionary choice: to blow up his own prison walls and live to tell about it.

If you think your own situation is far removed from Jiwe's, think again. His conflict is not unique to gang members or street soldiers. I can guarantee you that today there are many Wall Street high rollers grappling with the same identity issues and prison walls. There are many of you who are unhappy with your own lives because you feel you're someplace—in a job, in a relationship, in a circumstance—that you don't want to be in, one that does not align with the truth of who you really are.

We construct our own jail cells, whether it's an ordinary, everyday rut, an obsolete mindset, or a destructive emotional state. We have allowed someone or something outside ourselves to become our prison guard. Whatever issues prevent you from moving forward in life, you have to blow them up. You have to be strong enough to break through, and take ownership of the life that you truly deserve.

Inherited Quicksand

Jiwe's circumstances led me to a powerful revelation: many of us are stuck in what I call "inherited quicksand." In addition to the daily fears, doubts, and obstacles that plague us, too often we're weighed down by unacknowledged genetic and environmental sludge. It conspires to create an even greater disadvantage, making it even harder to escape.

Inherited quicksand is different for each of us. It may be your father's indecisiveness, your mother's negativity or rigidness, your homies' recklessness, your community's poverty—all the stuff you do, the things you believe, the possessions you want, habits unconsciously passed down—are the same things that have been plaguing too many of our families for generations.

By examining where he was, Jiwe was forced to blow up not only the things holding him back but the things that had destroyed far too many members of his immediate family. The revelation was this: in blowing up our own self-destructive stuff, we can save the lives of generations who are still unborn. Just like that Vegas casino poised for demolition, we can't settle for just removing one floor at a time or rehabbing the entire structure to get to the root of our problems. Literally, we must blow the whole building up and truly start over with a new fresh, hopeful foundation.

Whether our issues are generational or not, we all have them. Often we convince ourselves and others that "we just gotta deal with it"—which generally means "survive it." No! That is no longer an option. We actually must get rid of it. Dealing with denial and dysfunction, and pretending that certain things are okay that really aren't okay simply enable self-destructive thoughts and actions. That makes it impossible to reach that place that you were uniquely created to inhabit.

I am a firm believer that there are no accidents in life. I was invited to the Healing Starts With Us press conference as a spokesperson, and that allowed me to meet Jiwe at a critical time in both my professional and my personal life. Dramas and tragedies aren't the only impetuses for permanent change. The unexpected small moments—invisible to the world—are sometimes even more powerful catalysts.

Breaking Free

Jiwe's life is not the only story that proved to me how critical it is to break through. I was in the midst of another nonstop national speaking tour on college campuses. Day in, day out, whisked here and there, from plane, bus, and taxi to campus auditorium, hotel, and bathroom. My shoulders ached from lugging around laptops and luggage, from sleeping nightly on another strange pillow in another strange bed in another strange hotel room.

I'm not complaining, mind you. It's blessed work, and I'm always invigorated by the exuberant young crowds who come out to hear what I've to say or, as is often the case, to whom I come to listen. The rituals of my life on the road remind me how much we're all creatures of habit, and how so few of us have the courage to blow up our comfort zones.

I watch my audiences file in, and I notice how the seats fill up so predictably. Some folks head straight for the back row, while others cozy up in the middle of the auditorium. Then there are always those determined few who rush right up to be front and center. As they file in, most are unaware that where they seat themselves at my lecture is exactly where they sit at a concert, on the bus, in class, at church—and even in the movie theater.

I can't be too critical of this behavior because, as I make my way back to my hotel room, I recognize my own habitual travel regimens. How I often order the same dinner from room service each night, grab the same snack from the vending machine down the hall while I wait, and watch the same TV channels before I head off to bed.

It's not that we're boring or unimaginative as we rush to find our favorite seat in the auditorium or automatically order "cheeseburger and fries." When push comes to shove and we're introduced to something new, intimidating, or even exciting, most of us seek the comfortable position as opposed to the uncomfortable.

After all, it's so much easier to follow than to lead. Don't you feel this to be true in your own life? There are possibly fifteen different routes you could take daily to work, eat, shop, driving or walking, yet we often fail to alternate among them. Think about it: Baskin-Robbins has thirty-one flavors. How many have you tried?

Okay, so if this book is about finding and expressing your very best life, what do ice cream and your route to work have to do with it? you might ask. Simply: if you can't at least try a new way to work, or a new flavor of ice cream, how will you ever break down the very big, very real walls that separate you from becoming your personal best? In my life, I've found that it's not the big decisions that detour me as much as the hundreds of little decisions I don't make—like my fear of doing something differently. It's those seemingly small decisions—that deter me from reaching for something bigger, better, a bit scarier, and more rewarding. It's your fear of driving a new route to work, trying new foods, looking for a new job (especially in the current precarious economy!), changing careers to pursue what you really want to do with your life, even breaking up with the person you are with because you're really not into that person so much and you need to find who is right for you.

Therefore, driving a new way to work, or trying a new flavor of ice cream, are more than mere baby steps. Blowing up those small habits is preparation for life's ultimate challenges, and your ultimate breakthroughs. After all, the more little changes you make in your life, the more open and receptive you become to the bigger changes. And that may lead you to the biggest change of all—discovering who you really are.

So when I say try a new flavor of ice cream, do you really think I'm talking about butter pecan or pistachio? Hardly. I'm suggesting you start small to think big, even if it means changing just the smallest things in your life—at first. I suppose it's human nature to choose the comfortable over the uncomfortable. When folks walk into a bustling auditorium full of well-dressed strangers confronted with three hundred seats to choose from, they naturally lean toward the row that makes them feel the most at home.

The only problem is the old and familiar ripples throughout the rest of our lives as well—and with a lot bigger consequences than a seat in the back row or missing a few extra flavors of ice cream. I think of the colleague who always wanted to start his own business, but he never could justify the risk of leaving his cushy office job and all the security it afforded him.

I think of the many folks I know who always wanted to get that advanced degree but could never quite seem to find the time or money—or both—to go back to school and achieve their goals.

I recently watched actor Morgan Freeman play opposite Jack Nicholson in *The Bucket List.* His character, who knows every answer on *Jeopardy!* and could easily give Alex Trebek a run for his money, always wanted to be a history professor. Instead, he took a job as an auto mechanic when his wife got pregnant with their first child. When asked why he never went back to school in all that time, his response was, "Forty-five years go by pretty fast." Indeed.

I could go on like this for pages and pages, but I think you get the general idea. Therefore, I'm going to suggest that you learn to take a small leap forward out of the familiar and into the unfamiliar.

Look at your daily life, and see where and how you're spending your energy. Ask yourself: What are you doing? Who are you doing it with and why? Like Jiwe, to answer these questions, you'll have to face the hidden conflict between the person you are and the person you're destined to become.

Don't just move the pieces of your life around with clever shoulda, woulda, coulda to fit in new mental junk that's just going to have to be moved around in a few months or years anyway. Consider each piece of your complacency, and see if you have the courage to become a demolitionist and raze your old walls to make room for new life.

Now, I'm not suggesting that you quit your six-figure job, leave your spouse and kids, and join that reggae band you always wanted to. In this part of the book, we're going to be dealing with the habitual people, places, and activities that you've invited to help furnish your prison cell. These unquestioned bonds can hold you back.

Custom-Made Cells

The thing about our personal jail cells is that we build them ourselves: they're of our own creation, and they don't go up overnight. We spend years, even decades, crafting very intimate, very damning, and often custom-designed prison cells where we feel both extremely comfortable and, at the same time, extremely trapped. I'm not exaggerating when I compare the restraints that hold us back to a real jail cell, which keeps us from living our true lives as surely as the iron bars of a prison.

Many of us feel that we're in too much debt, too weighed down with responsibility, bills, or mortgage payments to ever break free. True, responsibilities must be tended to and bills must be paid. But before you give up on your life's dream as you sign that next car payment check, ask yourself, "Is it the money I make that's holding me back—or is it something else entirely?"

Before we go on, stop and think about the possible ramifications of blowing up an obstacle in your current life and breaking through to a new life, a new you.

Don't Live Your Life Mindlessly

Paul is a big movie buff who for years saw every hit movie, munching his way through every wide release Hollywood could shove down his throat: two, three, sometimes even four or five movies a week, to say nothing of $3 boxes of candy and $5 bottles of water.

Then one day, he forked over $8.50 for a small tub of popcorn and a medium soda, and it hit him. He was literally flying through money! Even worse, aside from gaining a few extra pounds every year, he really had nothing concrete to show for it.

That night, Paul went home and ran the numbers: four movies a week at $8 a pop came out to $32 a week. Double that to account for assorted snacks and sodas, and he was racking up $64 a week at the movies—sometimes more. That came out to $3,328 a year in his local cinema. Right then, Paul blew up the notion of what he was not—he was not a mindless consumer. So it was relatively easy for him to shift from watching first runs at the movie theater to watching movies at home.

Paul didn't quit going to the movies altogether—some films he just has to see on the big screen. But by connecting with his true identity, he never bought another $5 bag of Twizzlers. That may sound minor to you but three grand a year is not small change. Paul was beginning to make that first critical *Everything I'm Not* list, and that list is even better than Morgan Freeman's bucket list.

Ask the Hidden Questions

My point here is not that movies are bad or that popcorn is evil, but that there's always some place to save if you really, really think money is the ONLY issue holding you back from living your dreams, chasing your passion, and finding your true identity. As Paul's story illustrates, it's all in how you perceive things.

For several years, Paul thought nothing about spending over three grand a year at the movies. He did this not because he was extravagant but because he had never truly contemplated his identity and the amazing benefits that come when daily choices and actions actually align. Paul couldn't stomach the thought of "giving away" that money anymore when he recognized that part of his identity was connected to the idea that he was not "that guy" who wasted money on unimportant things.

He knew he needed to realign his thoughts and his actions so that they lined up with who he claimed to be. Suddenly, shelling out $20 a pop at the afternoon movies wasn't quite so harmless.

Most times, of course, money is not really what's holding you back from chasing your dreams or becoming your best self, but it's a convenient excuse. After all, it's much scarier to ask yourself who you really are and live with integrity than to postpone your inner dialogue and escape to the big screen with overpriced popcorn and a soda. Blowing things up and starting all over again is a lot more intimidating than simply moving things around so your life looks different. Blowing things up to catalyze a breakthrough means digging deep inside and posing unasked questions that need honest answers.

Successful entrepreneurs often discover that a key component of their identity is their ability to face an uphill battle every single day of their lives, to say nothing of uncertain paychecks and very little job security. This is true of entrepreneurs in every field, whether it's entertainment, politics, start-up companies, new inventions, sports, or the creative arts. The uncertainties they face would intimidate most of us. If we can blame putting our dreams on hold because "I can't switch jobs now, I'll never be able to afford it" or the "I need a job with benefits" excuse, it helps us sleep much better each night in that prison cell called nine-to-five employment.

To get comfortable with "who you are and who you're not," to really understand what you have to blow up to break through, you first have to know who or what you're afraid of. Everyone has issues, but those who succeed in life are able to face their issues. They make a decision to blow up the issues that are holding them back no matter what has to be done. They cultivate the necessary tools to break through their fears.

Are you willing to look at your unresolved stuff—your issues? Issues plague all of us until we make a choice to face them. Your issues can help you face what you're not. You are not your survival or money issues—blow them up. You are not your relationship or family issues—blow them up, too. You are not your employment or your educational issues—blow them up as well. When these issues are active, with no relief in sight, it can feel like you are your issues and that you'll never be able to break through to your true self.

So, before moving forward, pledge to yourself that you'll be open and honest about your issues. Give yourself this opportunity, perhaps for the very first time, to really dig deep and face not just your fears, but also your future.

Early on in my own self-exploration, I decided to find out who I was by taking a counter-intuitive path. I began my self-discovery not by asking "Who am I?" but rather "Who am I not?" This led me to new perspectives, awareness, and stepping-stones that I could easily have missed had I approached my self-examination in a traditional, linear framework.

Be Patient

These questions probably aren't new to you. If you're unhappy about something, chances are you're also pretty vocal about it. We all have friends we try to avoid, if possible, because they're such complainers. Usually their complaints are always about the same exact thing: money or the lack of it, relationships, jobs, work, or school, and even kids. There are many more questions to come in this book. These are just a few that are specific to show you what may or may not be keeping you inside the prison you've built for yourself.

Whatever jail cell you've constructed for yourself, you can break out of it for good, but not without hard choices, and not without a lot of hard work. As the plastic surgeon said to his patient when she asked how long it would take to recover from her face-lift, "It took you sixty years to look like this. The least you can do is give yourself a few weeks to recover from this procedure."

Therein lies the big problem with a lot of us today: we want our answers immediately, if not sooner. Blame technology, blame computers, blame the Internet, blame whomever or whatever you want, but the only solution is to convince yourself that you're worth the wait. Remember that you're the only one who can truly change your situation.

In this book, I'll never ask you to do something unsafe, unsavory, or unwise. But I will always ask you to look at every situation from a different perspective before you go back to doing the same things the same ways you've always done them. If you think about it, change is really the best solution for most of our problems. If you're unsatisfied with your life as it currently is, well, change is the solution you've been looking for. You just have to get over your aversion to change and expand your tolerance for risk.

If you want to discover who you are, you'll have to ask some major soul-searching questions along the way and find out who you are not. These questions are part of the "know thyself" edict from ancient philosophers that can help you probe and discover your identity right here in the twenty-first century. Your answers will offer essential clues that will help you discover the real you. Once you have a handle on these essentials, you'll be ready to blow up your prison and break through to claim the freedom to be your authentic self.

Remember, answer honestly. No cheating!

- Are you in prison?
- What are you in for?
- How did you get here?
- Who arrested you?
- Who is the warden?
- Who are the guards?
- Who testified against you?
- How did you get convicted?

- How long did you think you'd be in for?
- How long has it really been?
- Do you ever have visitors?
- Is there any hope of parole?
- Any hope of escape?
- Have you ever thought about breaking out?
- Are you resigned to living a lifetime behind bars?
- Can you imagine what it would be like to be free?
- What would it feel like to blow up your prison?
- What would the breakthrough to freedom feel like?

I Am Not My Parents

Parents can only give good advice or put us on the right paths, but the final forming of a person's character lies in their own hands.

— Anne Frank

Too often in life, we fail to become the person we were meant to be because we're focused on the person we're supposed to be. Today, I see scores of people riding on the same merry-go-round. It's not surprising. Most people are conditioned from birth to be the person someone else has told them they should become. This can be both positive and negative. I know a young boy demonized by his single mother for no other reason than because the little boy reminds her of the man who left her. The son is destined to carry the weight of a man he may have never known. On the opposite end of the spectrum is the boy whose father is a business mogul, a man who has ripped through corporate America to amass great wealth. The son finds himself trapped when he's forced to major in business despite his love of music because so many folks expect him to be his father. He, like many of us, has been encouraged or forced to take a journey that was never his to begin with. The problem is that this reality also makes taking his own journey very difficult.

Often people are incapable of taking a trip because they're weighed down by too much baggage. Similarly, it can be daunting to strike out on one's own, particularly when a family business or profession beckons with its safety, familiarity, and security. (Trust me. I know all too well what this is like.) Reminder: this book is about achieving and fulfilling your own unique, personal best, and no one else's. Throughout your journey, you'll face hard questions, questions you must answer for yourself, about yourself.

You are not your parents. You don't have to go into the family business to succeed—or become a doctor or lawyer just because your parents want "the best" for you. It's okay to pursue your best on your own terms. It's even possible to do it without burning family bridges in the process. Just remember, on the road to your personal best, you can't be successful if you're living out other people's expectations and continually trying to become their best instead of your best.

It's time to declare your own personal independence. Consider it your own personal Bill of Rights. That's right. I'm granting you permission not just to break out of the prison you've created for yourself, but also the prison your family and friends might have unintentionally created for you.

Before you can declare your independence and achieve your personal best, you must first go through the process of realizing everything that you're not. Only then can you become everything you are. To do this you must make three major (emancipation) proclamations.

I AM NOT MY PARENTS.
I AM NOT MY FRIENDS.
I AM NOT MY PAST.

It seems obvious: you can't be who your parents, family, and friends think you should be. However, it's not as simple as it sounds. As you recite these proclamations above to declare your independence, it's essential that you begin to consider the false identity that has you struggling to reach someone else's best instead of your own.

You Are Not Your Parents

The starting point is our parents. Parents are the single most influential relationship that you'll ever have, bar none. So much happens in this concentrated petri dish of parental influence that it's often difficult to separate how we see ourselves and what we desire from how they see us and what they desire. We base what we do on what our parents did, or, in some cases, did not do.

Regardless of a growing child's hopes and dreams, many parents try to live out their dreams—vicariously—through their child. They want to accomplish everything that they did not do through their child. (I have also seen many cases of children who attempt to do even more than their very successful parents did.) Sometimes this is the unconscious effect of "parenting on autopilot": the father who just assumes his son is into sports or the mother who enlists her daughter in ballet classes year after year because, well, that's how her parents raised her. Besides, what good daughter would not want to dance ballet? In either case, these children live in a kind of purgatory, unable to move forward. This happens far too often.

As a former youth pastor and national youth director for the NAACP (National Association for the Advancement of Colored People), I can't tell you how many parents I've seen attempting to live vicariously through their children. I've counseled many young people involved in activities they absolutely hated that required a serious level of commitment. What's especially painful is that often these kids are actually good at the activity and, if the pressure at such a young age had not been so relentlessly applied, they actually might have enjoyed it. Instead, they were faced with a thankless chore and a real opportunity wasted.

This is one of the most dangerous aspects of what I call "parental prison," cloaked in goodwill and disguised by success. There's the dad on the sidelines, cheering the son on; there's the son, shooting another basket, scoring another touchdown, striking out the opponent.

What could possibly be wrong with this picture?

Winning the football game, gaining entry into the college of "your" choice, or even being made partner in "the firm" can cover up the fact (often quite well) that you didn't do any of it for yourself. In reality, this is just an attempt to console a parent who happened to be less talented or ambitious or, in some cases, had fewer opportunities.

We all remember the guy in school like "Smitty." He was a decent pitcher who possessed above-average size and strength for his age. The opposing offense and defense shook in their cleats when faced with Smitty's strength at bat and the force of his pitch. The crazy thing was that no matter how well he played, Smitty never seemed to enjoy it very much. The reason was clear when he was not playing well, and explained why he played in the first place: his father's fearsome bellow from the sidelines.

"Smitty, throw a strike!"

"What the hell's wrong with you, Smitty?"

"Smitty, get a grip!"

"This isn't the girls' league, Smitty!"

All of which highlighted one blatant fact: Smitty was playing for the approval of a father who loved his son but had only half the ability of his son. There's nothing wrong with participating in an activity or choosing a life direction at the recommendation of a parent, but the question we all have to ask ourselves is, for whom are we doing it?

Other children have the opposite experience. They spend their lives trying to escape the curse of a negative parent. Think of the child in a single-parent home who has the unfortunate pleasure of looking like the parent who's no longer there, or the two-year-old boy who's labeled by his mother as "worthless" because his need to cry reminds her of her irritation with the child's father, who left them. I know young men who grew up in homes without dads, and from the time they were kids they were told that their fathers were nothings. Consequently, these sons spent their lives doing anything they could that would make them not their fathers.

Do you know how long it takes to wash the stain of "worthlessness" from your own skin? For some, it takes decades; for others, that childhood taint never quite comes off. There's the young man who's expected to be the star athlete, scholar, or millionaire businessman just because his father happens to be one. Or there's the prodigal daughter who never quite measures up to her older siblings. And of course, there's the "responsible" one, who always has to watch over the younger children, make them dinner, or ease their fears. Or the child of the alcoholic, the overachiever, the genius, the thug, or the self-indulgent parent.

These are extreme examples. Most of our parents do not fall neatly into any of these categories. Too many of us live somewhere in the middle. Too many of the life decisions we make in our developmental years are predicated on what Mom/Dad/another family member thinks. What do they think I should or will become?

Peter's parents—his mom is a cardiologist, his dad a sitting judge—fall into the first category. Throughout his entire upbringing, his parents essentially told him that he had a choice: he could become either a doctor or a lawyer. That was it!

They never relented. They constantly asked him if he was going to law school, or if he'd decided to go to medical school. He was on the receiving end of this kind of pressure from the time he was in grade school. In high school, the pressure became even greater. Of course, he had to have a summer internship, but his choices were either the hospital or the courthouse. Talk about options!

Because Peter was younger than I, I watched this from a different perspective. I could never recall his parents asking him what he cared about, liked, or had an interest in doing. In fact, I remember times when he told us that he wanted to join a bowling league or pursue his interest in playing football, only to receive their negative response. His parents always said, "You don't have time for anything else." He had to join Junior Achievers of America or participate in Jack and Jill, an upper-middle-class black social organization.

At a certain point, Peter converted. He told everybody that he was going to be a doctor and going to Xavier University in New Orleans, a historically black college that ranks first in the United States for placing African American students in med school, even above the Ivy Leagues.

Revelations come in different ways for each of us. For Peter, it came when he was a sophomore at Xavier and Hurricane Katrina hit. Only when was he forced to deal with this life-changing situation did he realize that he didn't want to be a doctor. It was at his parents' home in Charlotte that he started to figure out what to do now that Xavier was closed. He had lost everything. He'd been living in an off-campus apartment, and did not know when or how he was going to be able to afford to move back down. His parents were incredibly wealthy and paid for his school, but they insisted that he be responsible for certain things, and housing was his responsibility.

Picture it. There he is, sitting at home, thinking about what he was going to do, when he suddenly realized—and exclaimed right out loud!—that he didn't want to go back. He didn't want to be premed. Faced with choices—for example, other universities were accepting Xavier students—he did not even want to apply. Suddenly it was clear to him: the only reason he felt that he had to go back to Xavier was because his parents wanted him to go to medical school. He did not know what he wanted to do because he'd never given himself time to think about who he was. He had only been who his parents wanted him to be—which was just like them.

Because of the tragedy of Hurricane Katrina, Peter was able to tell his parents that he was going to do something different. The experience of surviving the storm had shown him that life was short, and it made him realize that he didn't want to go to medical school. He did want to make a living, and he did want to take care of himself. He would choose a respectable profession that both he and his parents could be proud of and tell their country club friends about, but he wasn't going to be a doctor.

Instead of returning to Xavier, Peter took a semester off and headed to New York University. His parents reluctantly accepted his decision. Ultimately, I think they were relieved that he'd remained focused and returned to school.

At NYU Peter met some friends of friends who worked on Wall Street. He changed his focus to finance. He was reacting against what his parents did, but not their values—again, he did want to make a good living.

Peter discovered that there were industries that would allow him to reach his financial goals and to continue to enjoy a comfortable lifestyle without doing exactly what his parents did. He made a very conscious decision, in essence, to reject his parents' professions but to accept their lifestyle.

Peter graduated and went to work on Wall Street. He does relatively well and enjoys what he does. Of course, considering everything that is going on today, everybody who works in finance is questioning what their future will be. Peter at twenty-something is still young enough to recover, and/or change course and pursue his personal best.

How to Tame Parents' Expectations

It doesn't have to take Hurricane Katrina, some other crisis, or a minor breakdown to disassociate yourself from your parents' expectations or your parents' lives. Start by making the following affirmation very clearly: "I can love my parents without being my parents." The best children, and sometimes even the worst children, are afraid of disappointing their parents. Therefore, they convince themselves that if they do something different from what their mom wants them to do, or if they go in a different direction than their dad expects them to, that means they don't love or appreciate their parents. Of course, that's just not true.

You can appreciate everything your parents have done for you. You can appreciate who they are. You can love them to death and still know that their desire for you to do a particular thing, like becoming a businessperson or lawyer or an underwater bubble blower, is ridiculous because it's not what you want to do. It's easy to forget, so you have to remind yourself periodically. You need to tell yourself that the real way to show your parents that you love and appreciate them is by using what they have done for you to become the best person you can be, not by becoming their clone.

On the other hand, if you grow up being compared to a "bad" parent, you don't have to try to prove to the world that you're not your bad parent. If you're not happy and you're doing something that you hate doing, the fact that you're living a lie is actually a slap in your parents' face. You're setting yourself up to ruin your life, not to achieve the things that you could.

Rectifying this situation does not mean you need to have an actual conversation with your parents, but you do need to have an internal conversation with yourself. If you want to have a conversation with your parents to make them feel better and to give them a clearer understanding of what it is you want to do, that's fine. But you can't have the conversation with them if you haven't first had it with yourself.

You Are Not Your Friends

Peer pressure is a beast. In college, students create cliques. Even if they're in different departments or different colleges, people often set courses during their undergraduate days that lead them to the same place. Sometimes the basis for these relationships seems contrary to what we say we want to do.

In my freshman year of college, I established friendships and kicking-it buddies. I ran with people who wanted to have fun, who wanted to party. I didn't run with people who wanted to be successful by studying. Conventional wisdom says that everybody in college wants to do well, but in reality that's definitely not the case. The people I ran with were not studying students. They weren't the ones who were trying to figure out how to achieve balance in their lives. They were the people who wanted to get drunk on Wednesday night. We excelled at throwing incredible parties in the middle of the week when other folks were studying. We partied almost every night of finals week. It was absurd.

Ahmed finally got to me. He partied and he hung out with us most of the time. But I never saw him during the day. When our grades came out, I was stunned. He got all As, except for one B. I had done terribly. When I asked him how he got such good grades while we were partying so much, he said, "Well, Jeff, you didn't think I was doing nothing during the day, and then kicking it with you all at night, did you?" During the day, he was studying, and studying hard.

That was an eye-opener for me. I realized the need to begin setting myself apart. I understood I could have a good time with friends, but I had to prioritize my personal vision and not the vision of that group. Often, we accept a vision of ourselves based on the group's identity instead of focusing on our own individual vision and instead of asking ourselves, "What do I need to do for me?" Only after you've answered this question can you make choices to support the person that you want to be instead of who your group wants you to be.

This experience also illustrates that sometimes we need to be courageous enough to do something different. Showing people through your actions is often a much better way to respond than simply saying something. Actions make an even stronger and more incontestable statement. Doing that, you often avoid burning bridges—I had plenty of opportunities to step away from my party clique and say or do something different, but I didn't. What is important is to remember that you can choose at any moment to live your life differently.

Speak the Truth

It's very important to communicate with your friends in a way that projects your vision and protects your friendship. At the end of the day, you're trying to bring everybody around to support your vision, not alienate them from you. Talking about how you feel and exploring your dreams and plans can be invaluable.

One such conversation I had when I was about twenty involved my best friend, Cliff. We partied together. We went clubbing together. We hung out together. We had a really good time together. Eventually, though, I realized that all we were doing was having a good time. Don't get it twisted—I did do more than kick it in college. But there was no depth or balance to our friendship. I couldn't tell you what Cliff wanted to do with his life. I couldn't tell you what his dreams were. All I knew about him was who he wanted to date and where he wanted to party.

The person who I called my best friend had no idea what I wanted to do or who I wanted to become. He had no inkling what my dreams were or anything else important to me. Therefore, he could not support me in them. The only things Cliff was able to support me in were those things actually preventing me from getting to those places.

I realized that if I wanted to continue this friendship, Cliff had to know me better and know what I wanted better, and I'd have to do the same for him. I had to sit down and explain that while I loved him like a brother, I couldn't remember the last time we talked about anything serious. I didn't mean sitting around philosophizing about politics or the evening news. Our serious conversations were really just superficial banter about current events.

At the time, my ambition was to go into politics, possibly even run for public office. I shared my dream about making a difference in our community and my desire to play a role in shaping grassroots policy. I wanted to put myself in a position to learn the things I needed to know and be more strategic in my networking. I needed a mentor. Because as it stood, I wasn't focused and was spending too much time drinking and hanging out.

Cliff felt where I was coming from. But he liked hanging out. It was fun. The timing just wasn't right for him. But it was right for me. Fortunately, we didn't stop being friends. To this day, if either of us ever needs anything, we can call on each other. Cliff accepted that we weren't in the same place and he didn't want to stand in my way.

Sometimes, when you realize that you're not your friends, things will change. You may not hang out as often. I didn't convert Cliff. He didn't say, "Let's take over the world." He wasn't ready for that. I could have lost a real friend. Luckily, I didn't. Cliff was a real friend and we stayed in touch.

You Are Not Your Past

No matter where you are now, it doesn't have to be your final destination. Things that happened in your past, especially bad things—something someone did to you, something you did to yourself, or the person you once were—sometimes play too great a role in defining who you are today.

Sandra was promiscuous from the time she graduated college until her mid-twenties. She dated as many men as she could, had sex with as many men as she could and, unfortunately, became known for her behavior. At one point, she embraced her sexual freedom as a badge of honor. The embrace became a trap when, at twenty-six, she wanted something more than superficial relationships.

Despite the problems in her social life, Sandra always had a good job and was incredibly successful. Now, however, she wanted a relationship that was as successful as the rest of her life, one that was meaningful and responsible, and one that the people she knew would respect.

Eventually, Sandra met Dwayne, who knew her reputation and didn't judge her. He really liked her. They began a relationship, but at first Sandra couldn't understand why Dwayne wouldn't sleep with her. He was demonstrating how much he valued her, but she wasn't used to this kind of treatment from a man. Instead of seeing his behavior as a compliment, she began to obsess about it and saw it as rejection. Sandra believed that men only regarded her as a sex object. Dwayne wasn't like those other men.

One day Dwayne told her, "This isn't about your past relationships. This is not about the person you used to be. Sometimes it bothers me that you have been with so many men, but you're not that woman now. Why don't you know that?" When Sandra shared her story, she admitted, "Dwayne allowed me to see myself in a way I never had before!"

Now married, Sandra and Dwayne are one of the most inspiring couples I know. They really enjoy each other. They're not perfect: they struggle with the same things all couples do, but they really love being together. They truly value each other. They have children who are thriving and happy because they're in an environment that's full of real love, compassion, and caring. They were able to create that environment because Dwayne saw more in Sandra than who she'd been, which allowed her to see that she was not her past. Once she let that image go, she was able to move forward and let go of all that shame and regret.

Sandra realized all of the things that she wasn't—she wasn't a whore, she wasn't innately promiscuous. She finally figured out who she really was: a monogamous woman in a meaningful relationship, a woman who could actually give and receive love. When she realized all the things that she was not, she was able to discover who she was. And you can do the same.

Think about the things that your parents are that you've embraced but that you don't like. Think about your friends and ask yourself which traits of theirs you've assimilated that make you uncomfortable. Think about the things you no longer are or no longer want to be. Once you've identified who and what you're not, you'll be ready to declare your independence, which comes with six "inalienable" empowering rights.

Your Bill of Rights

Let me emphasize that these rights are only tools to success, not a paint-by-numbers path to be slavishly followed. Parents, friends, and family can only lead us so far. Once you learn your rights, it's up to you to make them work for you.

I Have the Right to . . .

. . . Be Myself
. . . Create My Own Destiny
. . . Fulfill My Own Dreams
. . . Succeed on My Own Terms
. . . Be Recognized for My Own Worth
. . . Unparalleled Success

I Have the Right to Be Myself

As a parent it's great to see children sharing their father's talents and passions. When it's done right, when parents encourage their children to seek their own path and, with that encouragement, the child does indeed choose the parents' path—what a joy.

It's like watching Ivanka Trump becoming a businesswoman in her own right, blossoming under her father's tutelage, or reading that Will Smith's son, Jaden, is going to be in another movie—this time, without his dad.

As a parent myself (my oldest is ten), I look at my three children and see talents, gifts, and even desires that are specific and distinct to each of them. My daily personal prayer is that early gifting will not keep them from their own personal evolution—especially if that evolution seems impractical or makes little sense to their dad.

Growing up, I experienced the flip side of the coin when I faced my own identity conflict as a college freshman. My first year at the University of Toledo marked my eleventh year running competitive track and field. At that time, it was the single most important activity in my life. Seriously, my entire world revolved around track. From running with the Hopefuls Summer Track Club, where I really learned to love the sport, to the mighty Cleveland Heights High School Tigers, where I started to distinguish myself, I loved it all.

My parents supported my passion, but it was not something I did for them. By the end of my junior year in high school, I had no doubt that I would be recruited by some school, somewhere, to run track. Before the outdoor track season started, I was recruited heavily by some decent Midwest state and private four-year institutions. After choosing the University of Toledo (primarily because my father bribed me with a car), I prepared to have a full-ride athletic scholarship.

Once I got to the University of Toledo, however, I quickly realized that I wanted to do more than simply run track. I didn't understand that I had made the track a prison for myself until I tried to break free and do more than just run. My coach, of course, had a totally different picture of what my college life should look like—after all, his team was financing my education. At first I ignored him, but he did not relent. After several arguments about my involvement in campus service and leadership organizations, primarily the Black Student Union, my coach finally said he did "not bring me to the university to do anything but run track and go to class."

Finally, in my sophomore year, I realized that I had to make some real decisions about what I wanted my life to look like and that it was my responsibility to define myself in the process. This decision strained my relationship with my dad for about a year, but I believed I had the right to be myself. Then I became president of the Black Student Union and we put together a national conference with students from about thirty-five other universities, which, for Toledo, was a big thing. My dad attended the conference and at the end he expressed his proud support of my accomplishment, admitting that he had not been able to see what I saw for myself.

I Have the Right to Create My Own Destiny

You probably received one of the following three types of parenting in your formative years—nurture, neglect, or nepotism. Many of us may have experienced a combination of all three.

Whether your parents took painstaking efforts to provide you with the care necessary for you to become your best by nurturing you, or you were neglected and forced to make it seemingly on your own, or even if your parents practiced nepotism and gave you everything, requiring nothing in return, you still have a right to create your own destiny.

- Nurture prepares you, from childhood on, to understand the importance of decisions you'll have to make and the value of self-respect. If you're a nurtured child, your personal decisions have been encouraged, and you've been taught the meaning of respect, based on a sense of your own self-worth.

- Neglect comes with baggage that can weigh you down when you need to make decisions that affect your life.

- Nepotism gives you unearned opportunity and favored nation status, but it can leave you less prepared or unprepared when you must make choices of your own. This can lead you to become someone for whom personal accomplishments have no special meaning because you've been fed from the silver spoon of privilege and value very little except your own self-worth (or should I say net worth).

No matter how you were raised, today it's up to you to decide how to use these Three Ns to get what you want out of life. The decisions you make now will affect whether you live well—a life of your choosing, or poorly—a broken-down life not of your choosing. Many people still think they have to live according to their parents' script. Again, quite the contrary: you were created to build on what your parents did, not imitate it.

I Have the Right to Fulfill My Own Dreams

You were not born to right the wrongs or complete the unfulfilled goals of your parents. Parents can, consciously or unconsciously, build a prison for their children—a parental prison that their children must struggle to break out of if they're ever to fulfill their own personal best. Parental prisons can be damaging. You cannot live your life to complete what your parents did not. In the best-case scenario, parents are a blessing; in the worst, they can be a curse. Either way, you must be able to accept (as early as possible—the sooner, the better) that for better or worse, you're not your parents.

I Have the Right to Succeed on My Own Terms

You're not doomed to be in sales just because your father was a salesperson. You're not sentenced to be a stay-at-home mom just because your mother was. Of course, if you can't wait to be a salesman and are looking forward to being a CEO homemaker, more power to you. Just know that there are many more options available to you than those your parents chose for themselves, or may even have chosen for you!

I remember being about seven years old and thinking that the name "Jeffrey Ian Johnson" was the most "uncool" name ever. Simply because my dad was a Junior, I wanted my name to be "Johnnie B. Johnson III" instead. The third—and especially those three roman numerals—seemed really cool at the time. (Not so much anymore—things change.)

When I told my mother, she proceeded to tell me how upset my grandmother was when she and my father decided not to make me a namesake, to forgo the noble honor bestowed with a third title. My mother didn't want me to have the middle name "B," which was way too Columbus, Georgia (no offense to the Johnsons or Columbus, Georgia) for her first son. I believe my parents wanted me to have the chance to be my own person, and for that, and the nurturing they gave me over many years (and to this day), I am eternally grateful.

Many children are doomed before they know it: doomed by how they look, by how their parents think they look, or whom they may look like, by some skill (real or imagined) that they may possess, or even by how tall they are. Try being a six-foot-four black high school kid who doesn't play (or even enjoy) basketball. It's almost heresy! Now try being a four-foot-six white kid who loves basketball and can't wait to try out for the team. Impossible!

You're more than the sum of your parts, your "parts" in this case being the shared DNA handed down to you by your father and mother. What they gave you was the gift of life that's now yours to transform, to do something with—to do something you want to do. You don't have to earn it or owe them something for it or repay them. You're not an indentured servant, doomed to live out your days in your parents' shadows simply because you had the nerve to be born!

While I'm not so naive as to think that we're not at all affected by who our parents are or the environments in which we were raised, I do believe the premise raised in James Hillman's *The Soul's Code: In Search of Character and Calling*. Hillman asserts that no matter the environment, the soul was created to be independent and thus defines itself for itself. Break the mold, shatter the myth. Maybe your parents were poor; that doesn't mean you have to be. Maybe they never traveled across state lines; that doesn't mean you can't be a frequent flyer!

I Have the Right to Be Recognized for My Own Worth

It's not only the pretty, the smart, the famous, or the rich who get to reach their personal best in this life and live out their dreams. You're born with the right to achieve, the right to excel, and the right to be recognized for your own worth.

Maybe your parents put you down or did not build you up enough along the way to adulthood. Maybe they divorced when you were young and your father was not around to help you become the man you were meant to be. Maybe your mother smothered you, ignored you, or favored another sibling to the exclusion of the others.

I had a colleague whose younger brother was "the pretty one." His younger brother was tall, with wavy black hair and hazel eyes, and everything this sibling did was greeted with much fanfare, no matter how small or insignificant. My colleague worked twice as hard, not just to get attention but also to earn hard-won praise.

When my colleague got birthday or Christmas presents, they often related to his "station" as the "smart" brother: books, records, games, and the like—while the prodigal son always got designer duds and fancy cologne. In addition, the brothers lived their lives according to very rigid, very ingrained, very unrealistic guidelines set forth from birth.

So the younger brother grew up, let himself get out of shape, and lost his hair! No longer the pretty one, he floundered. What was his identity now? What could he do when the role he'd been groomed for all his life no longer fit him? The smart one grew up and out of his family and moved on to flourish in a world that accepted him not for how he looked (or didn't look) but for who he was, how he treated people, and what he accomplished, all on his own.

The lesson here, I suppose, is that we ALL have the right to be recognized for our own worth, regardless of the size of our shoes, the value of our bank account, the color of our skin, or which bathroom we use.

Remember, who you are today does not define who you'll be tomorrow. I can always tell when people are walking in the best lives for themselves. They may not be the best dressers or drive the hottest cars, but their sense of self-worth and satisfaction is so obvious that it's nearly overwhelming: they have dropped the mask and discovered the prize dwelling within.

I Have the Right to Unparalleled Success

You should be the greatest in your family. Consider that statement a challenge, one your parents would gladly have you accept. It can be challenging to dream beyond the horizon of the family business, your father's income, your mother's degree, your brother's failure, or your sister's shortcomings. Would you hold yourself back because of what others think, even members of your own family?

Sadly, the answer to this question is, all too often, yes. Many of us define our horizons based on history, family history. Dad makes sixty grand a year, Mom makes fifty, our older bro makes fifty-five, and his wife makes forty-eight. Over time, the sixty grand becomes our default measure of success. Not that sixty isn't good, or fifty or fifty-five or forty-eight. And if you're happy and can support yourself on twenty-eight grand—please teach us how.

We're talking about baselines, not borders. However, where do you fit into this equation? Does the security of your parents' lifestyle affect your decision to open your own business, invent something new, or branch out on your own? Can you see how the corporate mentality of those who surround us helps to squelch the entrepreneur in us?

It's never too late to live your own dreams. Gene Hackman didn't start acting until he was over thirty. The man who invented Cup of Noodles, Momofuku Ando, got his inspiration at age fifty. *Angela's Ashes* author Frank McCourt didn't publish his first book until he was sixty-six.

Why wait? The sooner you know that your parents want what is best for you, not to dictate the who and why and how you'll live your life, the better. Recognize which of The Three Ns you've been given. Many of today's most successful, powerful people—including former poet laureate Maya Angelou and media mogul Oprah Winfrey—suffered incredible neglect and abuse as children, but they drew on what they didn't have to create the very world they wanted.

If nepotism leads you toward your destiny, embrace it and appreciate the advantages given to you. Either way, your choice is yours.

If nurtured by your parents, encouraged and respected, then you've received the greatest gift of all. To waste it by settling for anything less than your personal best on this planet would be a crime of the highest order.

Everything I Am

We all grow up with the weight of history on us.
Our ancestors dwell in the attics of our brains as they do
in the spiraling chains of knowledge hidden in every cell of our bodies.
— Shirley Abbott

Children mature differently. Some grow up quickly, asserting their independence in early childhood or young adulthood. Some are still immature the day they graduate high school or college, or the day they enter the workforce. Frankly, some never grow up. Some cling too tightly to their mother's apron strings; others sever them altogether. Some respect their fathers too much not to join the family business; others hate their fathers too much to entertain the notion.

Once, a long time ago, I heard a sermon in church that has stuck with me to this day. A father took his son fishing. The boy was a terrible fisherman, and over the course of the day the boy caught not a single fish. Every instinct the father had said, "Catch a fish for the kid. Put him out of his misery. Just take his pole and catch a fish with it!"

He didn't. Instead, he patiently taught his son what kind of bait to use, how to cast his line, how to keep a finger poised—just so—to feel the first strike, how to reel the fish in slowly, not too soon, not too late, and how to sink the hook good and tight. The child grew impatient and frustrated, surly, and soured on fishing completely—until he caught his first fish! At that moment, all was forgiven, and even though it was late and the light was almost gone, it was all the father could do to drag his son home with his one little fish. Obviously, the son got much more than a single fish. He learned how to catch a fish—on his own and in his own time.

This is a simple lesson and one you've no doubt heard in various versions before. I like the story because it encapsulates a father's frustration: he wants to do so much for his children but when we force rather than teach—it doesn't work. So much of parenting, of teaching, is founded on trust—trust that the child or the student will learn to do the right thing at the right time.

Now is the right time for you. It is time for you to examine your relationships, to explore what your parents have given you, and apply it to your life, not theirs. There comes a time when every child must break away from hearth and home, and strike out on his or her own. Sometimes this happens early, other times later. Sometimes you can live away from home for a long, long time, never truly declaring your independence.

Think of all the adults you know who still have "parental" issues holding them back to this very day. Don't wait until it's too late to declare your own independence. Heed this mini Bill of Rights and realize that life is yours for the living, regardless of what your friends and family might think.

Traditional wedding vows state, "A man shall leave his mother and father and cleave to his wife." Whether you're male or female, gay or straight, young or old—consider the wisdom of this time-honored tradition. Embrace the rite of passage that is leaving your parents' side, either literally or symbolically. They didn't raise you to be carbon copies of themselves.

At birth, you were given certain inalienable rights—not just the few I've chosen to highlight here, but a lifetime's worth that we dishonor if we don't try to break the bonds established by society, our parents, our friends and, in most cases, by our very selves.

You've broken the chains that were holding you back and now you know your rights. The final step is to answer these three questions:

- What are you passionate about?
- What is good about you?
- What do you want to do with your life?

While the questions seem simple, they are a gateway to who you really are. What you're passionate about is a reflection of what you care about, what's meaningful to you, and what you're willing to live for. It's important to answer these questions because, for so much of your life, parents, friends, and experiences defined these answers for you. Get aggressive with these questions and tell yourself:

THIS IS WHO I AM. THIS IS WHAT I AM.

If you're not aggressive about your passion, how can you know who you really are? The things that are good about you make up your character. What you want to do with your life is also a reflection of who you are.

You cannot leave this chapter only knowing who you are not. That would be like pouring the foundation to build a home but never designing the rest of the house. Take your bill of rights, look in the mirror, and remind yourself of all that you can be. This will help you to acknowledge your whole self. Remember: everything you are not has led you to everything you can be—your best!

Chapter 3

I Am Whole

Now that you've shed all this historical stuff—the DNA of other people's projections that was blocking you from being able to break through to who you really are—there is a lump of clay on the table. It's waiting for a pair of wise and loving hands to shape it into the real you. Now you have the opportunity to forget your parents in the traditional sense. Yes, you love them. And in many cases it was their sacrifice that allowed you to get here. But in the last chapter you were able to declare emphatically, "I am not my parents and, more importantly, I'm no longer required to be. I have now claimed my independence. I am me." But what does that look and feel like?

Most of us, at this stage, don't know who we are. I mean who *all* of you—the whole person—is. Most of us know only those parts that we've spent our energies focusing on. Most of us have ignored huge chunks of ourselves. Some of you may not even believe that the whole you exists. To be your personal best, you've got to be able to create a complete picture of who you are. That means not just the employee, not just the parent, not just the athlete, not just the student or teacher, not just the singer, not just the friend. The whole, complete picture of you has to be developed if you're going to be able to achieve your personal best. This integration is the key to true personal fulfillment.

Am I giving you a headache? Relax. Together, we're going to look at that unmolded piece of clay and discover the hidden masterpiece that is you and you alone.

There is a whole you hidden inside the clay, a personal best now hidden from view. It's time to begin the process of acknowledging, accepting, and preparing yourself to embrace the best "whole you," not just the part(s) you've spent most of your life focusing on, to your detriment.

Discovering the "Lost" Self

To find the "lost" self, you have to be willing to identify the whole picture. Who am I in total, not in part? What are the things that make me? What are those things that I once truly enjoyed and somehow forgot along the way?

Many of us are prepared to be the best in only one, maybe two, aspects of our lives. That means that there are parts of your being you're neglecting, perhaps even entirely ignoring. Being your best in only one or two areas of your life is not good enough! All aspects of your life—parent, spouse, friend, sibling, boss, employee, student, teacher, and so on—all these roles are what collectively make you, the whole you.

My early focus on running track never kept me from looking down other roads. I was fortunate to have been involved in the church, speech and debate, family activities, and other opportunities that let me know at an early age that I was a multifaceted person.

You may not have been as lucky as I was to find those other things naturally and as early in life as I did. So it's important to take stock of the areas of your life that you've neglected, rejected, or simply ignored.

Stop right there! Some of you may be getting ready to skip over this part, believing you're not ignoring any part of your life. Stop, take a second, and be honest and open with yourself for the next few pages. Although it may not seem so right now, it's probable that you're ignoring a part—maybe more than one part—of who you are. So, stay with me.

Classic examples of people who excel in one area of life but ignore or neglect another are the high-achieving executives who never see their kids, or the people who make enough money to eat right and join a gym but still don't take care of their health because they're only focused on work, postponing those check-ups month after month. Many of us, regardless of how much or how little we make, do the same thing. If you're fortunate enough—accomplished enough—to make a lot of money, why not make the time to see your children? Why not make the time to eat well and take care of your body? Yet this kind of self-abusive behavior is common. I see it all the time.

Ty—although he makes a six-figure income—is always dealing with avoidable health issues. Most recently he has developed high blood pressure and high cholesterol. It's not because he has a hereditary condition or because he can't afford to eat right—he's just too busy to take the time to make lunch instead of eating fast food, and it's comforting to have a slab of ribs for dinner instead of a piece of baked fish.

Ty can even afford a monthly gym membership and the expensive market vegetables that many in urban communities do not have access to, but he won't make the time. Exhausted, he works ninety hours a week, and still believes his work is more important than his health. Ty is a wreck. His life is filled with manageable stress that could be transformed, he is a person who deserves to be whole, someone who is worth the effort required to live an enjoyable and full life.

Ty needs some coaching. After all, if he cannot make time for himself and his health, how can he possibly make time for his friends, his fraternity, or anything or anyone else? Ty the professional is actually killing Ty the person and that's not an acceptable way to live.

Solving Ty's problem is relatively simple. Some people don't need to do anything more than walk around the office during lunch, take the stairs, or choose something different from the menu. Ty could take ten minutes to make his lunch at night or in the morning to make sure that he is eating something he enjoys and is healthy for him. He could also hire a nutritionist to help organize his meals, or a trainer to push him to do minimal workouts.

The bigger question for Ty is whether his behavior is inviting other health risks and conditions. But until he acknowledges his personal needs, his life is going to continue to slip through the cracks.

Pay Attention

Number one daily life stresses? Spouses and kids. We often convince ourselves that we're ignoring our children and spouse when we're really ignoring the father and the husband or the mother and the wife inside us. In other words, not only those around you suffer; you also suffer by not paying attention to that role in your life that can give you joy, meaning, and fulfillment.

Some of us justify the neglect of those closest to us on the grounds that our work is what allows us to provide for them. You aren't denying your wife, husband, and kids because working fifty or sixty hours a week affords your kids the opportunity to go to private school, or allows your husband to buy the fancy car he wants, or your wife to buy whatever she wants. However, do you realize that you're also denying yourself the enjoyment of your partner, whom you loved enough to marry—a person whom you could spend your downtime with and really be a partner to? Do you realize that you're also denying the husband in you?

Let us pause here for a minute. I don't want any of you to miss this point. Many of us hate the pressure of a spouse or significant other who demands our time and attention. We get irritated with our kids because they have the audacity to want to demand our attention. However, most of us do not think for a moment about what we're missing. Do you realize that by not coming home and spending time with your kids, you're denying the father in you and denying yourself the joy of being able to watch your kids discover new things? Do you realize that you're denying yourself the ability to smile or laugh ten times more a day? If you realized all those things, would you still work fifty or sixty hours a week at the risk of killing the father, spouse, mother, and friend inside of you?

Psychologists say that every time you smile, you reduce stress. So just by making that one small change—by paying attention to that mother or father in you—and allowing yourself to smile more, you can reduce some of the stress in your life. In the end, it's about first processing those areas of your life that you were ignoring—the father, mother, husband, wife, or friend—and then recognizing what you're missing because you're ignoring those pieces of your life.

In a way, thinking about this makes you selfishly compassionate, because now you're thinking about what you're ignoring or neglecting from a selfish standpoint: you're considering all the benefits you'll derive from behaving differently. That's okay—because this new thought process also benefits everyone else in your life.

Learn to Embrace the Whole You

The unnecessary stress that comes from ignoring other aspects of your life is not only about ignoring family or friends—it's also about ignoring the things you love to do. These may be as simple as reading, or listening to music, or traveling. Often, when we're busy, we forget that those interests and activities made us likeable—more interesting, well rounded, and more human. One day, you finally realize that you thought you were working so you could travel more, but, actually, you work so much, you don't have time to travel.

You've ignored that side of you that made you feel human, that made you feel like more than "just an employee," more than "just a business owner." It doesn't matter what your work is or what level you work at. Some entrepreneurs believe "you eat what you kill," so they're always hunting, but even hunters stop hunting for a little while to enjoy the world around them.

You have to take a step back and remember those things you enjoyed doing before you got too busy to do them. Being your best is working your best, giving your best, loving your best, serving your best, and that translates into living your best. The key is to remind yourself how much renewed energy you get from doing the things you've ignored doing. Americans in particular are so caught up in work that we work until we become stale. We work so much that we're unable to be creative. We work so much that we're unable to be inspired. We work so much that we cannot come up with any new ideas. We excel in creating an environment that actually keeps us from being our best.

What in the world is productive about that? It's time to stop blocking yourself from being your best. You have to remind yourself that being in your most creative space is what allows you to work most effectively—to be your best. Even if you're concerned about being the best professional you can be, embracing the whole you helps you be that better professional.

Once you've acknowledged the other pieces of yourself, you can begin dealing with the practical issues. You know you've found the whole you when you're able to put together a picture of "all the pieces of me": the things that make you human, the things that make you the person you are, not the things that make you the professional you are or the parent you are. There's nothing wrong with compartmentalizing to get certain things done, but when you compartmentalize at the expense of ignoring essential parts of yourself, you end up being only the things you focus on and never the whole you.

There was a time in my life—in 2002 when I was national youth director for the NAACP—when I used the excuse that I was on the road all the time to get off the hook for ignoring other aspects of my life. Even when I was not on the road, but home in Baltimore, I ignored those same things. I was the first person in the office in the morning and the last to leave. I had a young daughter and a newborn son, but I was never home. I told myself that, as national youth director of the NAACP, I had an important position at an important organization and was doing good work. I told myself I needed to work hard so I could make money and advance my career, which would take care of my kids and ultimately do more for them than my parents were able to do for me. However, all of that was simply a rationalization. I was not being a good father, which was something my father was. I was completely neglecting the father part of me. When I had a free moment, I did not think to myself that I wanted to spend more time with my kids. Instead, I thought about how much more work I could do and with whom I could network.

Because I wasn't looking at the whole me, not only did I totally ignore the parent part of me, I ignored the spiritual part of me as well as other things I enjoyed doing—like riding horses, reading for pleasure, or going to the movies. The only part of me I didn't ignore was Jeffrey Ian Johnson, national youth director of the NAACP. How depressing is THAT?

I did not have a "road to Damascus" experience in which I was, metaphorically, knocked off my horse and completely changed, but I do remember a conversation with my daughter, Madison. She was three and a half years old at the time, and she was telling me about something she was going to do—a dance recital or a play at school—when she stopped and said, "I know you won't be able to be there to see me." She thought saying that would make me feel better—she was trying to show that she didn't expect me there, and that it was okay. She would not be disappointed when I did not come.

Suddenly, I saw that I had at worst ignored and at best neglected my daughter so much that she expected me to miss something that was important to her. She loved me so much that she wanted me to feel better. The realization forced me to ask myself, "What am I doing with my life? How have I gotten to a place where my daughter isn't upset about me not being there (or at least, she isn't saying she's upset). Instead, she simply expects me not to be there?" She has already accepted that I do not have time in my life for her, and she is only three and a half years old! I realized that was unacceptable to me.

Of course, I could not immediately quit my job, but I did start focusing more on the things that she needed and on spending time with her. For example, I immediately allocated every other weekend, no matter what, as the time we would be together. There were times when this worked and times when it didn't. However, my deliberate decision to be a better dad created opportunities outside of those every-other weekends. I visited her at school or accompanied the class on an extracurricular activity. What she said made me realize that I needed to be with my kids as much as they needed me. Even if that meant we were on the road together, no matter what else I was doing in my professional life, I needed to make time for them, because it not only was good for them, but it benefited me by making me a more whole person.

Fortunately, as time passed, I had more and more flexibility. I started working for myself, which let me tell myself when it was okay to stop working. In my unconscious days, I often told their mother, "I can't come pick the kids up from school, because I have to do this," or "I'm on deadline for that," or "I can't get away from this." Things like that happen from time to time, but now I tell myself I can stop working and make time for my kids. I had a hard time being a father up close. Now being a father to my youngest son Malcolm from a distance is one of the greatest challenges of my life. With each passing day, I realize the length and quality of the time spent with him connects directly to achieving my best.

Once I told myself I could stop working so much, I started making more time to do the normal things. Eventually, I started looking for those opportunities not to work and to spend more time with my kids. I know that not everyone has the luxury of working for themselves, but whether you have a nine-to-five or nine-to-six or even a nine-to-nine job, you still need to find time, and you can find time to do the things you want to do, to pay attention to the whole you.

There are still times—February in particular, because it is Black History Month—when I am incredibly busy. Nevertheless, I have made a pact with my management team that at the very least, every other weekend is a kids' weekend, so if I travel, they have to travel with me. Before my daughter, Madison, started first grade, I pulled her out of school for a week in February so she could travel with me. I arranged for someone to sit with her during my events, and we always brought books, coloring books, and pens, pencils, and markers. She was fine for an hour, sitting in the front row of one of my seminars, and I was able to spend time with her before and after the actual work time.

I did not go from ignoring one side of me to ignoring another side of me; I tried to find a way to ensure that I acknowledged all of who I was. The result has been a much stronger and more rewarding relationship with my kids now. Connecting to this aspect of me has required the most work, but it has yielded the most return.

There are always reasons to continue doing what you're doing, but you have to find a way to do something different if you're serious about making any kind of change. Whether it's buying a computer with a built-in camera and using Skype (which is free) so that your kids can see your face when you are talking to them—which makes a big difference—and you can see them, too, or writing letters and sending them things in the mail, the important thing is to keep in touch. Even though you are on the road, your children know that you are thinking about them. It is all about acknowledgment. It is about knowing that if I acknowledge this piece of my life, I have to acknowledge the things that make up that piece.

Identify All the Pieces of You

To acknowledge your whole self, you have to go through the process of remembering and identifying all of the pieces that make up who you are. It is important to write it down. Your answers will vary, but they might include things like, "I'm a worker or a professional, I'm a parent, I'm a husband," or "I'm a sister, I'm a mother, I'm a friend." This is the first part of the self-identification process. All of the roles must fit together to reflect the whole you.

Next, write down all the things you like to do. It can be as simple as listening to music, reading, sports, gardening, or traveling. Now explore these questions: What are the things that you loved to do when you were younger and what new interests have you abandoned along the way because you're too busy?

This is important. We not only ignore the various roles we play; sometimes we ignore even the things that make us better people. You can't ignore the things you need to do for yourself and achieve your personal best. You can be incredibly involved at work, be a great mom, but if you're not giving anything back to yourself, you'll never reach your personal best. That's why it's important to consider everything, including the things you love to do.

What Time Do You Waste? And How Are You Wasting It?

Once you identify all of your roles, and the things you like to do, you need to start being deliberate about how you spend your time. A daily calendar divided into thirty-minute segments helps you clearly see the things that you do, and all that you do not. Mapping it out helps you create an honest picture of how you're spending your time.

Many of us don't realize how much time we waste on things that don't really matter, only to complain about how little time we have to do the things that do matter. When you realize how much time you waste, you can figure out ways to use your time more effectively and start plugging in things that you have ignored.

There are creative ways to find time. Even stay-at-home parents don't spend twenty-four hours a day with their children. What do you do when they are sleeping? Do you watch some ridiculous TV sit-com or some cable news station that regurgitates the same stories over and over? Do you surf the Web, shopping for stuff you don't even need? All of us waste time.

So how do you shift that time to do something you would enjoy? You probably won't find the time to catch a flight to Paris for the weekend, but you can use your time to do something that gives you pleasure. As you begin this process, you may not be able to go to an art museum right away and take an art class, but you can go online and enroll in a workshop. Finding time is something you can do in stages, so the issue should not be "Where can I do this?" but "How can I do this?"

You can acknowledge the different parts of you in a number of ways. You don't want to pigeonhole yourself by only doing something as you have always done it, or only doing it as you once did it. Sometimes, because of very real limitations and challenges, you need to find a new way to do something.

Finally, it is unrealistic for you to go immediately from spending no time focusing on this part of yourself to spending a considerable amount of time focusing on it. This, too, takes time!

The Time Is Now

Another thing you can do to begin the process of identifying all the important pieces of the whole you is to give yourself thirty minutes in the middle of your day to write down all the things you want to do when you are not working or not doing the thing that takes up most of your time. This is the beginning of your "whole me" list of things you have ignored, things you haven't done, and things you would like to do.

Eventually, instead of giving yourself only thirty minutes to think about these things and write them down, you will actually do them. From Monday through Friday, you may have to stick to your normal routine, but identify at least one day a week to schedule an hour or two to just "do you."

From 3 to 4 P.M. every Saturday, there will be no cell phone, no computer, no text messages, and no e-mails. Instead, you will spend time with your kids doing something they want to do. If you are a stay-at-home parent, then find a babysitter, drop the kids off at Mom's. Focus on one of your other roles or desires that is important to you. Whatever you decide to do—make the time.

Keeping track of how your time is spent will allow you to reallocate your time. It lets you decide to take three hours a week and shift them elsewhere. It all begins with that initial acknowledgment. Now, instead of thinking about myself, I prioritize making time for my kids. I pick them up after school, creating time for their mom do something she enjoys.

You might love gardening, but you find yourself taking time away from gardening to work out at the gym. What you didn't consider is that gardening is a mild form of exercise: you're on your knees, using your hands, and moving around the yard. If you used to spend from 12 to 5 on Sunday afternoons gardening, you might now decide to garden from 12 to 2:30 and then work out from 2:30 to 5. This may sound simple, but it is amazing how many people don't decide where and how they want to spend their time and, therefore, never achieve their personal best.

Don't Let Your Life Fall through the Cracks

When I focused on work to the exclusion of everything else, I had no time to spend with my children. Madison said, "Daddy, I thought you said you were going to do this," or "I thought we were going to do that." I hadn't done the things I had promised. When Madison reminded me of my promises, I grew frustrated that she was holding me accountable. If I had simply paid attention, my three-and-a-half-year-old daughter would never have told me, "Daddy, but you said . . ."

Self-created stress can come from not taking care of yourself (as it did for Ty), or not finding time, or a way to pay your bills, or from neglecting relationships. Anytime someone says, "Hey, I thought you said you were going to do this. I thought you knew you were supposed to get that done." These comments upset or irritate us, but they're really the result of our own negligence, not because they are inherently stressful.

To avoid this kind of stress, you need to first acknowledge it. Then you need to spend the time required to keep it from happening again. Pay attention to the important things in every aspect of your life, so that the whole you will never end up falling through the cracks.

Acknowledging and addressing issues consistently makes you a whole person, without the stresses that come from ignoring, neglecting, or hiding them, and pretending that they will magically disappear.

See It and Believe It

Now you're poised to move forward and create a vision that is no longer about "How can I become the best boss?" or "How can I become the world's greatest mom?" It's about "How can I be my best?" However, you are not free yet because you must believe that you deserve the best and that it's out there waiting for you to claim it.

The journey toward your personal best is not an easy one by any stretch of the imagination. I have met countless numbers of brilliant people who are living mediocre, unsatisfying lives—not because they lack skills, intellect, or even vision, but because they fundamentally don't believe they deserve it. They are caught up in letting "everything that they are not" define them—you know, the mistakes, the challenges, the labels placed on them by other people that block them from seeing what their best actually is. They thought that greatness was reserved for people on TV or the famous, never realizing that because they were born, they have greatness within them.

Clearly, you cannot take the journey to greatness if you don't first believe in yourself and the possibility of change. You have to identify your personal capacity to do and be your best. If you commit to the process, taking stock of not only who you think you are but what you can accomplish, things like starting your own business, being faithful in a relationship, having the courage to make a career change, and following your heart's desire no longer seem out of reach.

No matter where your belief level is when this process begins, it's time to look in the mirror and say, "Yes, I can." I am not talking about President Obama. I am talking about you!

I know several people who have made it because they believed when it didn't make sense. We all know stories of people who pushed through and believed in themselves when it seemed like no one else did. Don't wait for someone else to give you the green light to start. God gives kids dreams of their own greatness. Often some "realistic" adult kills it. Believe big and begin now. So from Big Mama to Obama, you pick the story and ask yourself, "If them, why not me?" Believe you can, and you will!

Running on Empty

Many people have no idea they're on the wrong road to their personal best and have little faith in their capacity to get there. They don't know how to change lanes or move in a new direction. People from all occupations and lifestyles—from college students to successful entrepreneurs to top professionals, from the recently hired to the unceremoniously fired—are wrestling with the question of how to achieve their personal best. Even those who have achieved considerable success in one aspect of their lives can nevertheless remain unfulfilled.

The challenge of one famous hip-hop artist's pursuit of wholeness is a story that always sticks with me. RappR, who has enjoyed a decades-long, commercially successful career, is an indisputable icon. One day, we were sitting around the set talking. With all that he had accomplished in his music career, all the CDs sold, and all the music video awards won, I wondered what he thought his legacy would be. So I asked him. His honest answer was that "he had never thought about it."

Our connection created an opportunity, so we exchanged phone numbers. I didn't hear from him for months, and then he called unexpectedly. As we talked, he shared that, although he had achieved almost everything he wanted in his career, he had never taken time to develop other parts of himself outside of his work as an artist. Like many of us, he had reached a place where he longed to claim more wholeness. He wanted to make a difference but didn't know how to get there.

We talked seriously about how he could find a way to give more of himself. I asked what he cared about: Do you care about kids? Do you care about the environment? Do you care about your community? What's most important to you? Answering these questions will help you figure out how you can make a difference in the world.

After a green-light session, RappR decided he wanted to expose inner-city kids to new experiences—things like camping and the opera. He wanted to make sure these kids had the necessary financial resources, from scholarships to stipends. I suggested that he create a nonprofit foundation.

This was an opportunity for RappR to do things differently. One option we discussed was to do more than just perform in each tour city. He could insist that his team carve out time for him to drop by a school or a homeless center and talk to his fans. In addition to signing autographs, he could help promising young kids with their rhymes. It's a universal law: when you give of yourself, you always get something back but never in the way you might expect.

RappR liked the idea, and we began to put a nonprofit together. Lots of the ideas discussed didn't require any money but did require his time. The options were limitless and there was nothing holding him back—except himself.

I really wanted to support RappR, but you can't harness anyone else's dreams. Only RappR could make his vision a reality. Only he could will himself to become whole.

What's Good about You?

Some people know from an early age what they love doing and what's important to them, and nothing can stop them from doing it. On the other hand, many people have to come to grips with why they don't believe in themselves and their passions in the first place.

When I counsel people who feel stuck like this, we examine their family history, friendships, and other relationships. This helps them get a sense of why they feel the way they do about themselves. I suggest they ask themselves, "How do the people in my life feel about me?" "How do the people in my life make me feel about me?" "Do they support my decisions?" "Do they encourage and support me in a lifestyle that is constructive or destructive?"

It is essential for each of us to decide what we value, what is most important, and whether our values are in alignment with our dreams. You have to be honest with yourself as well as with the other people in your life.

Self-Value

Many people haven't really given any thought to what's most valuable about them. They're waiting for somebody to give them an acknowledgment or an award. That becomes the litmus test for their self-worth, rather than how they really feel about themselves. It is essential for each of us to decide what we value, what's most important, and whether our values are in alignment with our dreams. You have to be honest with yourself as well as with the other people in your life, if you're to know your true value.

Self-Value Inventory

Am I a good person?____

Can I become a better person?________________________________

Can my life in five years be superior to what it is today?________________

What do I think is good about me?______________________________

What don't people know about me?______________________________

Why NOT me?____

Often we force ourselves to choose only one side of who we are, at the expense of our whole self. As you'll recall, for the first half of my life, all I really wanted to do was run track. I started running when I was only seven years old. I remember the first competitive race I was in—at my mother's company picnic. I was in the lead when I looked to my side, and because I looked to my side, one of the other kids raced past. I said to myself, on that day—at age seven—that I'd never again look to the side when I ran a race. I did not, and I ran until my sophomore year in college. I loved track.

Track was the first thing that I was good at, and as a kid, there is nothing like winning medals and trophies. If that is not affirmation, I don't know what is. I'd get excited about every new medal, each new trophy, and would show them to my parents, relatives, and friends. They were proud, and I was proud. I was proud because they were proud. Still, it never became the sum of who I was. Although I was an All-American athlete, I knew there was more to me than track. I also belonged to a youth group at church, a bowling league, the speech and debate, and mock trial teams. That wasn't true of some of my friends, who immersed themselves in only one side of who they were—the athlete, the student, the actor. They had one thing they were good at, and damn it, that is how they were going to define themselves.

When you develop only one side of yourself this is how people will define you. This is how you will define yourself. This is how you will determine your own worth. That becomes a prison, because there are other parts of you that are valuable that you do not recognize. The inventory is an important tool because it forces you to stop and say: "Hold on, wait a minute, what are the things about me that are good? Am I a good friend? Am I a good son? Am I kind to people?" Most people never go through this process.

In a way, society encourages this. It no longer values the renaissance person. It expects you to be good at one thing, to specialize. It no longer values generalists.

It is not about all the things you are good at, it is about the things about you that make you a good person; there's a difference. You don't have win a "Friend of the Year" award to be a good friend. You don't have to be the kid who started his or her own business to be a smart. You don't have to buy your parents a house to be a good son or daughter. Being your best is not about getting a rave review. Being your best is based on this simple but powerful idea:

THIS IS WHO I AM
AND THIS IS WHAT
MAKES ME VALUABLE AS A WHOLE PERSON

PART II

ENVISION, EXPERIMENT, AND ENGINEER

Can You See It?

On the proverbial journey to your personal best, you cannot simply float through random space until you hit something, like Star Trek's Captain Kirk exploring outer space, the final frontier, or Christopher Columbus "discovering" the new world. You don't have that luxury. This chapter is critically important, because it guides you through the process of developing and fine-tuning your vision. Is your vision clear or is it just a blurry picture of what your best could be?

What Role Are You Playing?

You have to start by asking yourself, Where am I right now? Where am I at this very moment and what role am I playing? In the last chapter, you looked at all of the roles you play in your life. Now that you have this picture of the whole you, it's essential that you repeat the exercise for each of those roles you play and ask yourself questions about them. Do this for each area of your life because even if the questions are the same—your answers will be different.

Take a piece of paper and create columns across the top for each of the roles you play in your life—for example, business owner, organization member, parent, brother, spouse, friend, or any (and all) other roles you play. It's time to ask yourself some fundamental questions about how you're performing each role in your life.

Do You Show Up?

Suppose one of your roles is being a parent. What are the questions you'd ask yourself about how you perform that role? One question might be: Do I show up? This is relevant whether you're a single parent, married, divorced, or a non-custodial parent. I know parents who are with their children every day, and yet they're not present. There's no real interaction:

they don't talk to them, they don't play with them, they don't understand. They're just there in the house at the same time as their kids, but simply going through the motions.

You might say the same thing about your role as a spouse. You may be living in the same house, watching the same TV show on the same couch, but you stopped interacting a long time ago. You're more like roommates. Then there are those who are questioning their professional life. You've been going to the same job for five years. You show up at your office, but you're not truly present for work. You loathe staff meetings and count down the moments until quitting time, not giving even half of yourself to completing your tasks.

Do You Prepare?

For your job, answering this question may involve another question: Am I fulfilling the prerequisites and meeting the ever-changing responsibilities reflected in my job description?

For a parent, this question may mean: Am I preparing myself emotionally to spend time with my kids? Am I putting myself in the necessary mental space before I even come into a room?

George is an amazing dad. It's not that he does anything spectacular. What is spectacular is how much effort he puts into being a dad, how much emphasis he places on being a parent, how important this role is to him, and how consistent he is in parenting.

When he spends time with his children, for instance, he really thinks about the mental space he needs to be in when he comes home from work and walks into the house. So to put himself in that space, he listens to certain music, or he conjures up certain passages of the Bible that are meaningful to him, passages he remembers and knows and thinks about. These are ways he puts himself in the space his kids need him to be in when he walks through his door.

George understands that, whether he's had a stressful day at the office, a bad day, or even a great day, he could all too easily focus on work when he gets home. However, when he walks through the door to his castle, he consciously decides that he's going to focus on how his children's day was and to be present when one of his kids tells him, "Daddy, I skinned my knee," or "My best friend was mean to me today," or "I didn't do so well on my math test." When George walks into the house, he has fully prepared himself mentally, emotionally, and spiritually to be with his family.

Often when we think about being our best, we think about all of the physical things we have to do. For an athlete, that typically means that you have to work out, that you have to train. For an employee, that may mean you have to prepare by reading a particular document or reviewing a memo, or researching an important issue. All of these tasks are necessary to prepare for those roles. However, there are also other roles we play in our lives that require equal preparation, but the preparation may be much more emotional, intellectual, and spiritual than physical. It's important to recognize that some of the roles we play require that we reorient both our heads and our hearts.

Are You Investing?

Are you willing to invest the necessary resources to get the most out of each role you play in life? After all, one principle of investment is: "The more you put in, the more you potentially get out." But that doesn't mean you know how much, when, or even if you'll get a return. So really ask yourself, Are you ready to invest?

Risk is inherent in the investment process—whether it's a financial or an emotional investment—because there always are variables outside our control that may mean we'll take a loss. On the other hand, keep in mind that you can't max out on the back end if you haven't maxed out on the front end.

My friend Tanika is a great example because she wholeheartedly invests in her role as a friend. Tanika is probably one of the most healthily invested friends imaginable to her intimate circle. When I told her I was exploring new media opportunities on MSNBC and CNN to increase my exposure, while still working with BET, she was thrilled. It was great news for me, but at the same time I was concerned about the amount of research necessary to be on top of all the issues I'd be addressing. I was concerned about my energy levels because I'd always have to be up. I was thinking about my appearance because I knew my looks would always have to be tight: the stations always call at the last minute and I can't go on TV with my dreadlocks looking crazy without my image-conscious friends calling and fussing me out.

Anyway, from the minute I expressed my concerns to Tanika, I started randomly getting ties in the mail. She was sending me neckties! At first, they just showed up with general notes, but after I received the fourth necktie, she sent a lovely note that said, "You told me you were going to be doing more and more TV appearances. And a guy can never have enough ties."

Here was an individual so invested in being a friend, so willing to invest in who I am and what I'm trying to become that, without even being asked, Tanika said to herself, "My friend is going to be on TV more and more. He needs to look great, all the time, and a guy can never have enough ties. So just in case he's not thinking about this, I'm going to think about it for him." This was a very meaningful gesture to me. There are places and times that Tanika has been there for me in far more profound ways, but this was a touching example of her investment.

Tanika is this way with all her friends. She sends a card or a small gift for every one of my kids' birthdays, every Christmas, and every Easter. Moreover, she does this with everyone in her small circle of friends, not just for one "best friend." She is this thoughtful all the time, for all the people who are important to her.

Tanika's actions demonstrate "I'm willing to invest. I'm willing to give the best that I have because I care about these people." Moreover, she's not looking for any tangible "return" on her investment beyond the friendship itself. She's not looking to get something back, tit for tat, in return.

In fact, it's just the opposite, at least in my case. Half the time when Tanika calls me, I'm tied up. Although Tanika and I have managed luxurious face-to-face visits only a handful of times in recent years, she accepts me as I am. I'm not the type of person who remembers everyone's birthday or who checks in just to chat. And Tanika's okay with that, because she knows that whenever she really needs to talk to me, or really needs my advice or support, I make sure that I'm there for her. She knows I'm self-absorbed. She knows that I'm all over the place, trying to keep too many balls in the air. But she also knows that she'll always be guaranteed the best of Jeff when she needs it.

There have been times that Tanika has challenged me. She has called me on my behavior on more than one occasion, when I've completely fallen off the radar. She has said, sternly, "Friends don't disappear from each other's lives. I know you're busy. I know you have a lot going on in your life. But I deserve better." That gets my attention, because Tanika is such a kind person and she never reprimands people unless they truly deserve it—and I did. Still, she never expects me to respond to her investment in me in the same exact currency.

What's important to remember is that, in any one of your roles or relationships—as an employer or employee, as a parent or spouse—both parties have agreed to invest. Therefore, both parties have a responsibility. What Tanika calls to our attention is that it's important to protect your investment by "fulfilling your responsibilities." Each of us needs to do the same, in every role that we play in our lives.

What Is Your Attitude Now?

Investing in your relationship roles is important but your attitude may be even more important. Attitude determines outcome. Far too often, we want things, but we don't go in with a positive attitude—whether it's in a personal relationship, on the job, or with a particular project.

William—like many of us—says he wants to go places and do things, and he says he wants to be in a relationship. Yet I have never met anybody more negative. I mean, the sun can be out with not a cloud in the sky, and it's seventy-five degrees, with a perfect, pristine breeze, yet if I say to William, "It's a beautiful day," his response is, "It's not warm enough." We all know someone like William: there is a naysayer in almost everyone's life, whether in your family, your circle of friends, your workplace.

William is simply never in a place where he's very happy. His job is never good enough. He has been divorced three times. Much of his dissatisfaction has nothing to do with his capacity to have what he says he wants. Most of his disappointment and unhappiness have to do with the attitude he brings to the roles he plays in his life.

Managing your attitude is a daily challenge because a wide range of people, places, and things affect it. Ask yourself what your attitude is and why you have the attitude you do. William has never really faced his bad attitude. There are some family issues and some unfinished psychological business. Nevertheless, he believes his attitude is justified. People have challenged him on this idea. However, he believes that he *is* his attitude and that he doesn't have the ability to change it.

Almost everyone has some tragedy or challenge in their lives: nothing goes right for everyone all the time. Many people have chronic illnesses or disabilities. Or they have problems with their work situation or paying their bills. Others face tragedies in their lives: the death of a husband or wife who was serving in the military, severe injury of a family member in an accident, or raising a child with disabilities. Many people feel entitled to their bad attitudes.

So our first reaction to someone dealing with a difficult situation is, How could that person possibly be happy? Under similar circumstances, I'd probably feel bad, too. However, for every person who defends against pain with a bad attitude, there is another person in crisis who maintains a positive attitude about their situation.

Attitude is a projection of what you want and of where you are. There are people whose attitudes are a reflection instead of a projection. When I counsel leaders and young people in particular, especially those who are working in the community or on campuses,

I always emphasize this point. Your attitude should be a projection of what you want, not a reflection of what you're dealing with. For example, if you're a leader (at work, in your religious community, in your family, or anywhere), and only reflecting what's around you, then you can only be as effective as that environment. That's often not very effective!

I'm not suggesting that you should be phony and pretend you have a positive attitude when you really don't. Instead, I'm encouraging you to create the reality you want instead of wallowing in a space that reflects what you don't want. Acknowledging the reality of where you are and projecting the attitude of where you want to be are the necessary one-two steps for cultivating a good attitude.

Sometimes, an attitude problem is so serious that the person may need counseling because coaching and self-help can go only so far. Encouragement and coaching are good first steps. Counseling is an important second step—whether you get it from a teacher, a parent, or a professional. This can help determine if there needs to be a more serious intervention. When there are psychological barriers that require professional counseling, as in William's case, the best help one can offer is compassionate and caring support.

Attitude Shift

Nicholle wanted to sing but surrounded herself with individuals who couldn't see her vision. Subsequently she found herself in a rut. Looking for a change so she could live her dream as a singer/songwriter, she began the process of weeding her environment and her friends. After months of tedious work and laserlike focus, Nicholle was writing Grammy-nominated songs. Her entire life turned around.

She was able to make the attitude shift because she had already prepared and she had already invested. The only thing blocking her manifestation was her attitude. As soon as her attitude shifted, her journey started on a completely different level. Instead of being in New York, with people in the music business who did not believe in her, she decided to forget about the naysayers and the non-supporters and to plot her own course. As the old adage says, success really is the best revenge. Today, more and more people are coming to Nicholle. They're interested in her unique sound and her personal best—not someone else's.

Changing your attitude helps you eliminate the naysayers in your environment. Your attitude either attracts people or pushes them away from you. Sometimes, you don't have to end a negative relationship—a conscious shift in attitude creates an energy that people can either deal with or not. Let them decide what they want to do after you change—that's not your problem. In Nicholle's case, her attitude shift put her in a place where naysayers could not stay around because she refused to be limited by their negativity.

We can use Nicholle's best practices to learn the importance of creating the best attitude possible, fueling your attitude with positive energy, and rejecting naysayers that second-guess what you see.

All of these best practices can support you in manifesting your best and the attitude that's needed to get there. "Attitude determines altitude"—and how fast, how far, and how great you are is built on the attitude you bring with you. A positive attitude is the last step before you actually begin to manifest your vision. If you haven't prepared yourself, or invested in your roles, or do not have the right attitude, then you're setting yourself up to seek what you'll never be able to find. So suck it up. Get ready to roll. Your best is waiting!

The Jump-Off Point

Can you remember when you were a kid at a swimming pool, dreaming of jumping off the high dive, only to get to the top of the ladder, look over the edge and freeze up, punk out, get scared? Too many people who are no longer kids dream of reaching their personal best and fulfilling their heart's desires—but then fall short because they fail to start, punk out on life, or become scared of success.

The jump-off is dedicated to giving you the power to look over the edge of your own personal journey—and then jump. What is funny about the high dive is that the hardest part is climbing up the ladder and standing there. If you have been reading this book and actually pushing yourself to change, then you've already done the hard part here, too. Part I has prepared you for this very important moment. Yet if you fail to start right now, you'll never be able to finish.

The biggest killer on the journey to your personal best is fear. To reach your destination, you'll have to learn how to embrace fear and turn it into fuel to power your journey. Of course, it's unrealistic to think that you'll go through life and never be afraid. The key is to embrace your fear and use it to move beyond what has kept you standing still. Too often, we focus more on the fear of moving than we do on the fear of standing still. Even more terrifying is the thought that nothing will change. At least when you move—even if you fear that the worst will happen—there is still potential for change.

Throughout history, the people who've taken the leap when others stood still are the ones who've changed not only their own lives but have also often changed the world. Therefore, my goal is to push you forward. My method may offend you, but get over it. My intention is to prevent you from having to take that descent of shame, down the high-dive steps, and past the people who'll witness you giving up before you even start.

Are you beginning to get the picture? If you want to get to the next chapter, let alone the next step toward your personal best, you have no choice. Jump!

Take the Plunge: Accept and Manage Your Fear

Many people try to convince themselves that there's something wrong with being afraid. Fear may be an irrational emotion, but it's also a normal one. Even irrational fear doesn't make the fear any less real. My goal is not to tell you shouldn't be afraid; it's to show you how to manage irrational feelings. To do that—and this may sound strange—you can't be afraid of being afraid.

There are times when I'm so full of fear, apprehension, or anxiety about what to do next that I get pumped with adrenaline. Some people get that adrenaline rush as they wait their turn for their first skydiving experience. In my case, the adrenaline rush came before my first appearance on *Larry King Live*. It was inauguration week, millions of additional viewers were watching the news to see what was happening in Washington, D.C., and now I had a chance to appear on CNN's flagship show. I'll admit it, I was nervous!

Many people feel the fear when they have to face an audience and speak, whether it's a meeting with the boss, a PTA meeting, or a professional conference. Most people are fearful whenever they face a new situation. No matter how benign it may seem, it can still be terrifying. However, if you acknowledge your fear, and leverage the adrenaline rush that you get from it, it can carry you through a potentially difficult situation.

One night during inauguration week the call came inviting me to appear on *Larry King Live*. My publicist, LaVenia LaVelle, called to say that Larry was doing a show on President Obama, and he wanted me to appear and comment. Of course, this invitation didn't come out of nowhere. I had already been on CNN's *Headline News, The Situation Room with Wolf Blitzer*, and *American Morning*, so producers from those other CNN shows had seen how I handled myself on the air.

In fact, I'd been on probably a hundred shows before, and I've had my own TV show, but when I got the call from LaVenia, I confess, I was thinking, "The number of viewers watching me tonight on *Larry King Live* will be huge. I'm going to be appearing with will.i.am and Arianna Huffington—both of whom I know—and when the viewers see me, they're probably going to be thinking, 'Who's this guy in the tux with the locks?'"

I'd be lying if I didn't experience some anxiety about that. It wasn't that I felt I didn't deserve to be there. My anxiety was about how I'd perform. Who wants to bomb on *Larry King Live*? Had I, for a moment, allowed that fear to take hold of me and direct me, I would never have been able to do the show. As I waited to go on, I kept telling myself, "Okay, Jeff, you've done this a million times before," but I was still a little nervous.

The difference between managing fear and running from fear or denying it is that when you manage fear, you accept that it's there. I had to reassure myself that fear was in the house. So what if I was nervous? What mattered was what I planned to do with that feeling. Would I continue to worry about my nervousness, or spend the next ten to fifteen minutes before airtime focusing on three things that I was going to say, no matter what Larry said?

Inauguration week. There were three relevant points about Obama that I wanted to make. So I knew that whatever question Larry might ask me, I could answer, "You know, Larry, I think that's a good question, but what's more important about Obama is..." and then make one of my three points. By doing that, I harnessed my nervousness, and prevented myself from being in a position where I would answer on the fly, out of anxiety. I could have done that. Yet, taking the time to prepare a couple of relevant responses put me into a personal best space, where I could respond on a level commensurate with the other guests. I could demonstrate the level of sophisticated commentary that the people watching *Larry King Live* expect. If I had denied or ignored my fear, I'd have been sitting there telling myself that I wasn't nervous, or berating myself with thoughts like, "What's wrong with you? Why are you so nervous?" Alternatively, I would have simply focused on the fact that I was nervous, which would only have increased my fear. Neither of these reactions would have helped me step into the studio and do what I needed to do.

Fortunately, Larry asked reasonable questions like, "How is Obama going to affect the African American community? What do African Americans think about him? Why is this important for the country? What is it that we're getting ready to see?" These were all topics that I've talked about before, so my fear and nervousness weren't warranted. I was prepared. My fear was a response to the opportunity, and my preparation was a response to the fear. As I was leaving the studio, Larry said to me, "Jeff, I can't wait to have you back again. You were a great guest." Score one point for Jeff, zero for fear.

The jump-off is all about managing the fear—accepting it, realizing it's there, and then figuring out how to handle it. For so many of us, the jump-off never happens because we're so consumed by fear that we never figure out how to jump. We just stand still.

Fear Can Push You Forward

Too often, people maneuver themselves out of the jump-off with self-defeating talk. They've never accepted and managed their anxiety. They've never harnessed the adrenaline rush and pushed themselves to make the jump.

Terrie Williams knows the power of putting anxiety to work for you. Terrie was the first person to give me a consulting job after I left the NAACP. She allowed me to help her build her youth organization, The Stay Strong Foundation. Terrie always said that if she didn't wake up feeling a certain level of anxiety, she knew she hadn't challenged herself. So many of us don't realize that the fear and anxiety we feel is our body telling us that we're in the right place to be challenged. Yet, I don't know anybody who's reached their personal best who has not felt some level of fear or anxiety.

Life's breakthrough moments do not surface without a challenge. Even if you're pushing yourself, you may reach a point where you acknowledge that you're overwhelmed, wondering how you'll accomplish the task before you and if it'll work. When that fear kicks in, it can sometimes block you from taking the risk of leaping off the high-dive board.

When you reach the place in life where you have nothing left, you have nothing to lose. Fear is sometimes as basic as whether you'll be able to eat or not. It's all about survival. It's very tangible. It's in your face.

When you have a job, even if it's not a job you like, it's still a job that's paying you. When you're offered a chance to jump off and try something that'll take you to another level, you may lose something in the process.

At twenty-nine, Jamal Bryant faced this kind of challenge in his life and knew that there had to be a next step for him. Preaching from the time he was a kid, Jamal came from a legacy of excellence in ministry. Jamal's mother was a preacher and respected theologian. His grandfather was a respected pastor and his father is the presiding bishop of the AME (African Methodist Episcopal) church.

Jamal had hoped to continue in his family's tradition as he waited for the church to find the right opportunity for him. Despite his outstanding credentials, every single opportunity that he thought might happen didn't. The caliber of church he wanted was not available, nor would church officials be willing to offer him a small congregation in an obscure town. As a result, he was still at the NAACP as the national youth director, wondering what he should do next. Then his fiancée suggested that he start his own church.

His first reaction was, "What are you talking about!" Did she understand what it would take to start a church, the level of sacrifice required? And what would happen if it didn't work? Reality had taken hold—the fear of jumping off the diving board, and the possibility that he might fail.

Jamal had never been a traditional preacher, and the only reason that the AME church had tolerated Jamal's non-traditional style was because (a) he was the son of a bishop and (b) he was incredibly popular. Although he could easily wait for something to happen, he realized it might take a long time. After a great deal of prayer and conversation with his parents, Jamal knew that personal best was clearly connected to a call to develop his own ministry.

When he decided he was ready, he climbed the ladder. He stood on the board alone because he was no longer willing to compromise himself. He finally realized that he could either stay in his comfortable job, where he had a national platform, or he could jump.

He didn't jump off to his father's best or his grandfather's best, because neither man had ever started a church. None of his preacher friends and acquaintances had ever started their own churches in the way he envisioned his.

Jamal began to hold prayer meetings in his home, with forty-three people who were committed to helping him start this new ministry. He assembled a team that would help build his church from the ground up. Empowerment Temple held its first service on Easter Sunday in April, 2000 and twelve hundred people showed up.

In the first four years, membership grew to more than six thousand people. If Jamal, one person working alone at the beginning, had not decided to jump off he'd never have reached his personal best.

Failure

By now, some of you may have realized that you've never even attempted to acknowledge your fear and therefore have not managed it. If you're one of those people, I want you to look in a mirror right now. That's right, don't just think about doing this, but actually put the book down, go to a mirror, and look at yourself in that mirror. Then I want you to say these four words: "I am a failure."

That's right: "I am a failure." I'm not going to pump you full of optimism and positive thinking by telling you that you're a great person, or a faithful friend, or a loyal son or daughter, or a wonderful parent, or successful in your work, or that you can be all that you want to be. No matter how much you've achieved, no matter what you've been able to do in some area of your life, the fact that you're not willing to challenge yourself to get to your personal best makes you a failure. You've failed to produce what it is you've been put on this earth to produce. You might be the CEO of a small company, you might be a football star, or you might be America's best mom, but if you've failed to acknowledge and manage the fears that have stopped you from pushing yourself to your personal best, you're still a failure. In addition, you need to admit that to yourself before you can change and truly become your personal best.

Some of you may not understand this. If you failed to be the best father you can be, even though you already are the best businessperson, you're a failure. If you've failed to be the best son or daughter, community member, or teacher, even though you may excel in another area of your life, you're a failure. Remember how, in Chapter 3, you acknowledged that you're a whole person? Well, if that's true, then you can't accept success in one area of your life and failure in another and not acknowledge it.

Now that you've acknowledged that you're a failure, the most important question is this: Do you want to continue being a failure?

Do you want to continue not being the best father, or not being the best professional? Do you want to remain a failure that does nothing? On the other hand, do you want to risk temporary failure and do something to change your life? Do you want to achieve your personal best? If you do, then you have to jump, because you have no other option.

I can guarantee that you'll always be a failure in one area of your life if you don't do anything. However, if you're willing to jump off, I can guarantee that even though you'll make some mistakes along the way, you'll be further along on the road to achieving your personal best than you would be if you did nothing at all.

There have been times when I've said this to somebody, and that person has recoiled. "What do you mean, I'm a failure?" or "I'm not a failure: I've got more money than you do." or "Where do you get off?" Each time I hear this, I tell people they should be upset about what I just said. Let's be honest for a minute. Just because you're successful in one area of your life doesn't mean you've achieved your personal best. Until you challenge that notion, then you're always going to be great in one area and substandard in another. The moment you accept the fact that you're a whole person, you accept responsibility for being the best whole person you can be. Otherwise, your life is like a car that has the best and most amazing sound system—but no engine. You might have super-powered Bose 89 speakers, surround sound, and DVDs dropping from the roof, but if your car has no engine, you can't go anywhere, and what's the point of that? Are you really going to be able to enjoy your music while sitting in your car that can't move? I don't think so!

If your personal relationships are failing—if your marriage is failing, if your relationship with your children is failing, if you don't feel yourself anymore, if you can't find new things that you love doing—then you're a car with great sounds that's just not moving.

I've been known to piss people off, but that subsides when people realize that it's my job to challenge their complacency. I can recall doing a church workshop, designed to challenge traditional notions of manhood. One of the church board members, Mr. Pope, a very successful businessperson, decided to sit in just to see what I was doing. He thought he had everything together in his life: he had a beautiful wife, two kids in private school, a five-bedroom house, multiple cars, a great closet full of beautiful clothes, and a substantial savings and investment account. He was living the American dream.

Yet in talking to him and hearing from people close to him, I learned he and his wife were not happy in their marriage, and his kids seldom saw him so there was little quality time. Mr. Pope was very happy at work, but standoffish and irritable everywhere else. At work, he'd created a safe environment where he thrived. There, he was a superstar.

At the workshop I challenged my audience. "All of you who don't jump are failures." Mr. Pope immediately rose and said, "Where do you get off telling us that, young man?" He was pissed. Then he added, "I'm not even registered for your workshop, but I'm sitting back here saying to myself, 'How can you tell these men who are all trying the best they can that they're failures because they don't jump?'"

I answered, "Because you've invited me here to do exactly that. Now are you willing to become part of this workshop and acknowledge where you are a failure?" To my surprise, he said, "Okay, if that's what it's going to take for you to answer my question, I'm willing to listen."

Mr. Pope owned a successful software solutions company. I said, "That's fantastic. Are you turning a profit?"

"Last year, we made more than ten million dollars," he replied.

"Great, congratulations! With that, obviously you spent a hell of a lot of time running your business." This line did not go over that well at the church.

He said, "You're absolutely right. I don't know anybody who works as hard as I do." When I asked him, "When was the last time you spent a full day with your kids, without a cell phone, computer, or BlackBerry?" he looked at me as if I were crazy. "What the hell does that have to do with anything?" His response didn't go over so well either.

Mr. Pope was about to say something else, then he stopped to think for a second. I appreciated that he was honest enough to admit that he never thought about failure. He would have never viewed himself as having failed his family because he provided such a luxurious lifestyle for them. However, when he reflected for a moment, he recalled his wife saying, just the week before, that she didn't need more money. She needed more of him because there were things only he could do for the children, just by his presence.

Nevertheless, Mr. Pope still didn't regard himself as a failure. But by my measure, in fact, he was a failure because he failed to do anything about what his wife had asked of him. I'm sure this wasn't the first time his wife had expressed her dissatisfaction with him as a partner and as a parent. Mr. Pope failed to acknowledge his wife at all. Instead, he simply rationalized his actions.

Many of us have been guilty of this kind of rationalization. We justify our dysfunctional behavior because it allows us to maintain the lifestyle we've created. The truth is, working smarter, not just harder, managing your time, and acknowledging the whole you won't prevent you from earning money, running your business, or being good at what you do. But working smarter can allow you to stop ignoring the things you say are truly important. If you say that other pieces of your life are part of who you are, but you don't work to be your best in those areas, then you're failing yourself and you're failing the people in your life.

After the workshop, I talked to the pastor who was also present during the exchange between me and Mr. Pope. He mentioned that Mr. Pope and two other men had created a support group for busy dads. They began to create opportunities to help dads learn how to be more involved in their children's lives. I had planted a seed that seemed to be taking root.

Wherever I lecture or give workshops, there are some people who'll totally reject my message because, again, my approach isn't designed to make you feel good about what you're not doing. I'm not willing to celebrate the fact that you can plan a dinner, when people don't have jobs. I'm not going to support an awards ceremony and reward people for fulfilling positions instead of truly changing lives, any more than I'm going to hold a training workshop that celebrates a person just for showing up, before they've done the real work.

Admit Where You're Weak If You Want to Be Strong

Some people accuse me of being negative or full of tough love. My approach is to highlight what you're not doing and then begin to provide recommendations for what you can do. Too many of us allow an accolade or a pat on the back to remove any sense of urgency. You may tell yourself, "Well, I don't really need to push that right now because I'm doing great here." That's not really the issue: wherever you're succeeding, I guarantee, that's only one small aspect of your life. You need to work toward your personal best in every aspect of your life.

You need to have that sense of urgency in the areas where you're weak if you ever want to reach your personal best. This is not about how you can become the best CEO, how you can make a million dollars a year, how to navigate the waters in corporate America, or how to become the executive director of the best nonprofit organization in the world. Instead, this work is about:

How can you become your best person?
How can you become your best self?

That means you have to challenge the areas where you're weak right now, otherwise, you run the risk of continuing to do what you're doing, because it's a lot easier to focus on the areas where you're doing well than to pay attention to the areas where you're not.

I'm an agitator. It's my job to stir things up. I want to poke and prod you, to show that you can do even more. Good is not best, and that is the issue that you must continue to deal with.

I had an opportunity to speak to government employees working in the area of corrections: caseworkers, social workers, and correction officers. Because they work in a highly stressful environment, we discussed how important it is to have a release valve, and the necessity of developing some very real, enriching, and fulfilling personal relationships. That's especially important for people who have to cope with such incredibly stressful jobs, day in and day out, so that they don't go into work every day ready to kill somebody—and so they don't go home ready to kill somebody.

I started challenging them about their roles as parents, and one woman became very defensive. She said, "I'm a good mother. My kids are clean. I go over homework with them. I make sure that they eat. They don't want for anything. How dare you say this is an area all of us need to focus on? You don't know us." What was interesting is the fact that she said she was a good mother—when just three minutes prior, she said she thought she was a great correctional officer.

Was she saying that she thought she was great at work, but only good at home? I want to see you being your best in both. If being a "good" mother is good enough for you, then fine, don't do anything different. In addition, if you think those inmates at the prison deserve more from you than your kids do at home, then you're perfect and you don't need to do anything different. However, if you realize that your kids at home need as much from you if not more than the prison inmates, then you have to do something different.

This woman didn't want to hear anything else from me. Nevertheless, I understand I don't have the power to convert everybody and not everybody converts at the same time, in the same way. Part of helping people by sharing my best practices means being willing to plant seeds, and that somebody else may have to water them and shine some sunlight on them. People need different kinds of stimuli at different times in the growth process.

I've seen this happen. Two years ago a man in his early twenties came up to me and told me that when I spoke at a leadership workshop at his high school years ago, he thought I was full of shit because one of the first things he recalled me saying was, "All of you are not going to make it, not because you don't have the potential, but because all of you are not going to make the choices necessary to make it in life." Needless to say, his response was, "Who the hell is this dude coming in telling me that I'm not going to make it?" He just ignored what I said.

After he left high school, while running with the wrong crew and hanging out with the wrong people, he was with some guys who robbed a store. Although he was only driving the car, he ended up going to jail.

His first night in jail, that very first night in prison, he thought about what I said: "All of you aren't going to make it, not because you don't have the potential, but because you'll choose not to." He admitted that those harsh statements I'd made when he was still in high school were finally sinking in. He had plenty of time to think about what I said, because this young man spent two and a half years in prison before he was released. While in prison, he started reading, and deepened his personal relationship with God.

When he saw me again, he told me, "Jeff, I decided I wanted my life to be different. That was the thing that I didn't hear when you spoke. I heard you say that we were not all going to make it, but at that moment I could not process the rest of what you said. When I decided to be my best, my life changed. I didn't want to be around the same people. I didn't want to do the same stuff. I got sick of myself. That didn't mean I got perfect overnight. I've still got my shit, but what I was uncomfortable with has changed." The young man has enrolled in community college and is involved in his little girl's life. He hadn't been out that long when I saw him, but he's started his journey.

Be Honest with Yourself

Although some people may not think it's appropriate for me to stand up in a high school auditorium and tell kids who may already be having a hard time and living a hard life that they are going to fail, I tell them this—and I tell you this—because it's the truth. Our kids today are told all the time, "You can be anything you want to be. Every one of you can become president of the United States." The reality is that not all these kids make it in life. They don't all graduate. In fact, most urban schools in America have a 50 percent dropout rate, so clearly, not everyone is making it.

However, until we start to be honest with people about the reality of where you are, to face the reality of your errors and to recognize what's needed to change them, then nothing will change. If I go in with a "rah, rah, rah" message, I'll only make kids feel good about what they're not doing. Instead of saying, "Yes, you have the potential to be Barack Obama. You have the potential to be even better than he is. You have the potential to be even better than Condoleezza Rice or Hillary Clinton," my message is that if you don't choose to give your best, if you don't choose to surround yourself with the right people, if you don't choose to do the work that's necessary, then you're not going to get there.

I want to be honest with kids, I want to be honest with the people at my workshops, and I want to be honest with everyone I meet. That's why I say to you, reading this book, that you need to be honest with yourself and admit that you have all the potential to be your personal best within you now, but what you do with it is what matters. Don't just tell yourself, "Maybe I'll do something different next week," or "I'm doing okay for right now, so I'm just going to maintain."

Don't just maintain. Jump off!

Build Your Team

You've jumped. Okay, now what? Who's around you to help you out of the water? Who does your team consistent of? Unbelievably, our "relationship accounts" are not so different from our various bank accounts. In life, we have some relationships that add to our existence and others that subtract from our value as human beings. When you add more than you take away, your bank account balances out. Taking away more than you add leaves you unable to cash the checks you write with your full potential.

Choosing a team that can push you to be the best is a difficult task, one that many people—in fact, most people—would rather avoid. Let's start here: I've never known a sport that is as equally individual and team-oriented as auto racing. For those of you that aren't NASCAR or Formula One fans, we see the NASCAR drivers constantly in commercials, on billboards, and on products, but the drivers will be the first to tell you that without a good team in the pits, they can't even get close to victory lane, let alone sit atop their car and drown in the winner's circle champagne.

This is important because that's often how life is for the rest of us. We're clearly the drivers going full speed ahead. We're the ones who turn right or left and know when to brake, when to shift lanes, push hard, and thread the needle, or lay back and wait for an opening ahead.

Individually, of course, we're the ones in the cockpit of that car with the sole responsibility of getting it across the finish line. No matter what the crew does in the pit, we're the ones who have to have the instinct, the drive, the power, and the know-how to steer that car where we want it to go. However, throughout our lives we all have pit chiefs in our ear telling us what's ahead in the environment and how to work with the constantly changing road conditions. The pit chief tells us when to bring the car into the pit or when to push the limit and stay in for another critical lap.

Throughout the important races of our lives, we also have the pit crews who put gas in our car and change tires in record time. They do essential things like wipe off the windshield so we can see a little better and retain the vital homeostasis required to perform at our peak potential.

As any NASCAR fan will tell you, although Jeff Gordon or Danica Patrick may be standing on the hood receiving all the accolades in the winner's circle, they wouldn't have air in their tires or cross the finish line without the pit crew and the pit chief.

Therefore, I ask you, "Who's on your team?"

Choosing a team that'll push you to your best isn't the same as choosing a team of people who all want the same thing, or a team of people willing to support your endeavors. Choosing a team that'll help you to achieve your personal best requires a formula and the discipline to allow each player to do his or her job and really push you. You need a team with players who have different and sometimes contrasting personalities and gifts. The team must include the:

- **Enforcer:** Tells you the truth, regardless of the situation.
- **Listener:** Provides an open ear, if needed, and a shoulder to cry on, but most important, doesn't judge you.
- **Chess Player:** Knows the next six moves you must make to succeed and is always ready with a countermove.
- **Risk Taker:** Sees opportunity wherever it may exist, even in the smallest cracks—which is super valuable!
- **Spiritual Guide:** Provides prayer, meditation, a message, and a reminder that there is a power greater than you.
- **Elder:** Offers wisdom, wisdom, and more wisdom.
- **Free Agents:** Fill all your other specific needs on demand.

Choosing Your Team Members

In my own journey toward my personal best, I had to learn the most effective way to interview prospective team members. I want to share those best practices to help you identify and use your team most effectively. Remember, the team is responsible for pushing you through your journey to your personal best—even when you may not want to be pushed.

Having the right people around you, who are dedicated to you and invested in your future, is essential. You have to accept that you can't succeed all by yourself. You have to put together a team that can actually help you get there.

My buddy Paul has been incredibly supportive of me and my dreams from the time I met him in high school. Not long after I started appearing on television on a regular basis, we were having a conversation about my personal life, when he suddenly shifted gears and told me how great it was that I was working on a documentary. I interrupted Paul and clearly told him I didn't need him to be a fan, I needed him to be a friend. It was the first time in my life I had said this to someone I cared about.

Paul looked at me in a way that revealed his discomfort. Initially, he thought I was being totally arrogant. But when I explained that while I appreciated the fact that he supported my career, what I needed was somebody who knew me well enough to tell me when my stuff stinks and challenge me to move in the right direction. In other words, your team members should not be a team of cheerleaders. Instead, they need to be people who know you well enough to speak frankly during a particular leg of your journey.

This idea grew out of my own personal experience. I realized that no one person could be everything to me. In my own life and in the lives of people I have known—friends or people I have coached—I've seen people look for a confidante or consigliore, and they want that person to be everything. They want that person to be their cheerleader. They want that person to be their coach. They want that person to be their trainer. In some cases, they even want that person to be their lover. Again, they want that person to be everything, but as I said, one person can't provide everything you need. Each person has a certain set of gifts, skills, or insights that can help you grow in specific areas of your life. Therefore, you need to surround yourself with an entire team of people who'll push you in different ways to be your personal best.

When choosing your team, think of it this way: once you know what your vision looks like, and where you want to go in life, then it's time to become the casting director of your own movie. I'm an obsessive movie buff. I absolutely love movies, and in general, I like movies with great scripts, but I also like movies with a great cast because a movie with a great cast cannot be all bad. Each cast member creates a character that contributes to the quality of the whole movie.

The same thing is true of your team. You have to create a cast of characters that can fulfill your vision, the story that leads you to your best. It's important to focus on the entire cast. Concentrate your efforts on getting the right people around you, the ones that can help you maintain your personal best. This kind of thinking about best practices for team building led me to develop the following descriptions of the seven essential team members. Let's look at each one of these individually.

The Enforcer

The Enforcer is the most important member of your team because you're not always going to want to hear what the big "E" has to say. This person is probably the most difficult to keep around and, in many cases, he or she will rub you the wrong way. They're going to hold a mirror up to your face, and keep you accountable. Be assured they're going to say all those things that you don't want to hear. The Enforcer will tell you the truth, no matter what the situation, whether you want to hear it or not.

For example, Will Smith tells a story about going back to Philly after he won the first American Music Award for hip-hop. He had the award with him, and he was beyond cloud nine. He walked into his grandmother's house to show her the award, but before he was able to say anything, she said to him, "I need you to run to the store to get some sugar." She was reminding Will that, no matter what he had achieved in the music world (and later, on TV and in the movies), he was still just a regular person.

That story doesn't necessarily fit the "tough-guy" image of an Enforcer who has to slap us around occasionally, but, believe me, Will's grandmother was definitely Will's Enforcer. She was the person who reminded him who he was whenever he started to believe his own press, or think he was extra special or above reproach. The demeanor of your Enforcer does not matter as long as that person is someone who'll remind you that you're regular people and what your responsibilities are. Here is another example: judging from press reports, Michelle Obama may be the president's Enforcer.

The Listener

Listening well is an art—and a gift that most people do not possess. Most people I know pretend to listen only to figure out what they're going to say next. By contrast, a true listener is someone who actively listens, but doesn't necessarily feel the need to respond. A good listener takes in what you're saying, really hears and processes what you're saying. In some cases, when the person knows you well enough, they're able to listen between the lines, because listening isn't necessarily just about what you say; sometimes, it's about what you don't say.

There are times when you just need someone to hear you without responding or being judgmental. Sometimes, you just need someone who'll simply be a sounding board for you—and that's very important because that allows you to hear yourself talk. Hearing yourself say things out loud can lead to a revelation without the other person ever saying a word.

When you know that someone listens intently, it encourages you to say more. That's the other reason The Listener is so important. Nothing blocks a conversation like the feeling that the other person isn't really listening. There's no encouragement to go deeper, or to be more transparent and open, if you don't feel the other person is paying attention.

The Chess Player

The Chess Player is the person who's always looking four, five, and six moves down the road. Chess Players have the ability to see what other people can't. They understand point and counterpoint: that your decisions and actions in your life aren't only about what you're going to do next, but also about the multiple responses inherent in every decision you make.

These people are calculating, and sometimes it's frustrating to deal with Chess Players, because they never give you a black or white answer. If you ask a Chess Player, "Do you think it would be a good idea if I leave this job?" the response is likely to be, "Well, I don't know if it's about good or bad because, if you leave this job, then this might happen," or, "If you leave this job three months from now, it would be very different than if you leave this job tomorrow." Their responses are never cut-and-dried because they understand that multiple moves and variations of moves always exist, and that each has its different consequence.

In addition, the Chess Player is the most difficult person to find, because most people are not taught or encouraged to be strategic. If you're not a Chess Player, it's especially important to find one to help you on your journey to your personal best.

The Risk Taker

The Risk Taker sees the smallest opportunities, and is willing to try to make it through those tiny cracks to create a larger hole. When all the odds are against it, the Risk Taker believes in it, and he or she is willing to step out. You have to listen to what Risk Takers say with a grain of salt. After all, just because your Risk Taker wants you to take a risk in some area of your life doesn't mean you should take that risk. One of the reasons you need all the members of your team is that you often need to weigh each against another and find a balance for what's right for you at that time.

The Risk Taker is the one who helps you see things you might normally miss. Your role is to balance the Risk Taker with the Chess Player, because the Risk Taker may present an opportunity that has the potential for a high return, whereas the Chess Player will present the consequences that might occur because of making that move.

The Spiritual Guide

This person is also difficult to find, because by "spiritual," I don't necessarily mean religious. The best candidates for this role have dedicated their lives to the quest for inner peace, and they do very practical things—such as breathing exercises, praying, meditating, or simply listening to nature—that remind them that there's a power greater than themselves.

There are many beliefs, faiths, and processes, but even those who believe that the universe created itself usually believe that there is a force greater than themselves. Such people believe that whether the universe was created through a Big Bang or some other force of nature, that nature created itself. They may not belong to any organized religion, but they do understand that there's a language of the universe, such as the waves speaking to them when they sit near the ocean.

The Spiritual Guide can help you see the signs around you that get lost in everyday hustle and bustle. I believe in God, and therefore I understand that God has created everything around me. Consequently, I've been ministered to by simply sitting at the edge of the ocean and listening to the waves come in. I have received revelation, gotten big ideas, and achieved a greater sense of peace, simply from listening to the waves.

In contrast, a Spiritual Guide who's not religious might tell you, if you were facing a difficult decision or if you were in crisis, "Come on, let's take a walk on the beach," or might suggest that you let yourself take some time in silence. There is revelation in solitude. There also is an opportunity to hear yourself think—away from your cell phone, BlackBerry, the television, the radio, your iPod, or your computer. Spirituality is just about connecting to the spirit, to that innate part of who we are that's above and beyond the physical, that helps manifest ideas, creation, revelation, all of those things that, at certain points in our lives, are incredibly important. You don't have to be religious to do that: in fact, I know many religious people who don't know how to exist in silence.

Therefore, the Spiritual Guide's role is to ground you, to center you, to give you a way to seek knowledge or an answer from what created you, whatever you believe that is.

The Elder

The Elder is that sage who, from personal experience and observing the world, is able to give you very pragmatic advice. Sometimes, the Elder's knowledge is the result of mistakes that person made and learned from; sometimes, it comes from being a student of life and the fact that the Elder has witnessed and observed many different circumstances and experiences, some that were his or her own and some that were other people's.

There is a difference between Elders and old people. Elders understand their inherent responsibility to use the things that they've experienced and to place their hands on someone younger to help that person not repeat the mistakes of the past. In contrast, an old person is somebody who's simply lived a long time but who feels no such responsibility.

Also, keep in mind that it's not enough to simply be mature or have "an old soul." The Elder is truly older than you are, and therefore has the wisdom that comes from experience. You will need this person, too, to be part of your team to help you achieve your personal best.

The Free Agents

Finally, we have the Free Agents. You may need none, or one, or more Free Agents. To know whether you need a Free Agent, you must first determine if there's a specific need that none of the other six team members can fill. If so, you must determine what that position is and what you need from the person filling that position.

In my own life, when I look at my Enforcer, Listener, Chess Player, Risk Taker, Spiritual Guide, and Elder, one of my Free Agent positions is the Soldier. I need somebody with me who can fight—figuratively or literally. I need people with me who know how to soldier, who aren't afraid of the fight, who will look for the fight that's required to bring about the result that I need. I need to know that when I'm in the trenches, that person will be in the trenches with me; that when I charge and attack, that person will be right there with me, ready to attack. And because I have lived my life the way that I have, and haven't shied away from conflict but instead have tried to chart new courses, I need people who can soldier with me.

However, not everybody needs a Soldier. Once you've identified your vision, and identified that whole picture of who you are, then you'll be able to say, "Here's the free agent that I need." You yourself may be so much of a Soldier that you can go to war by yourself, but you may not know how to be diplomatic. You may not know how to calm things down or how to talk to somebody without the conversation becoming antagonistic. You may have so much fight in you that you create fights unnecessarily. In that case, you need a Diplomat in your corner who can calm the waters that you stir up.

Again, if you know your destination, and you know the whole picture of who you are, then you know what you need. Normally, putting this team together is about identifying people with character traits that you don't have or that you need to have strengthened. At first you may find it a bit daunting to think about how you can assemble such a team. This is especially true for those of you who feel it's hard to find just one good friend or confidante. Still, these roles need filling, and occasionally you can find one person who might fill two or three of them.

In my life, my father is the Enforcer, but he is also a Risk Taker, and he is an Elder—my father fills three of these roles for me. You don't necessarily have to have one person fill each of these roles; instead, you simply need to find people who care about you who have the skill sets you need to help you on your journey.

Finally, you may not need to have every member of your team working at the same time. There may be times when, for example, you don't really call on your Listener for a year. It's all about the journey; it's about having the tools you need as you progress down your road. You may go for two hundred miles on that road and not need certain things. Still, you need to know that you have this team in your circle, so that when you do need them, they're available.

How to Find Your Best Team

I first realized that I needed a team around me when I was in college. One day, I was sitting on the steps of the Student Union. It was late in the day, the sun was setting, and it was a Friday, on a commuter campus, so there were not a whole lot of people around. I was feeling down, because an event that I'd planned had not gone the way I wanted it to go, and I felt very alone.

Sitting there, I thought about whom I could talk to other than my family, and I couldn't really think of anybody. "I know I'm not the only person out here who feels like this. If I don't begin to build a team I'm going to just give up, because I can't complete this journey alone."

This is when I identified the different roles I needed others to help me fulfill. I hadn't yet identified the people; I only focused on the roles. Today, I have an amazing team. In addition to my family, I have a very close-knit group of friends, including my best friends, Jamon, Shaun, and George. My team members have rotated into different positions at different times and that flexibility has been a great asset.

My brother Jamon is one of the most laid-back people I know, and he's definitely one of my Listeners. He is not the Enforcer. He is not the Chess Player. He is not the Risk Taker. He is not the Elder. He definitely is the Listener. At times, Shaun can be a Spiritual Guide as well, but more than anything else, Shaun is a rock and my best Free Agent. He'll always be on my team. No matter how bad he's feeling, what's going on in his life, or what the situation is, I never have to look for Jamon. That is incredibly empowering because even if he can't do anything, he's there. Sometimes that's all I need, and it's often what we all need: just the comforting presence of someone who believes in you.

My friend George is a Chess Player. In any situation, George goes through a series of strategic questions, such as "What are your options? What will happen as a result?"

Of course, relationships are always in flux. So keep in mind that the people in your life may not always be available to play their designated position. You're changing and so are your team members. Therefore, the roles they play in your life may change and evolve. First, you have to know what you need, because if you don't know what you need, you can't create the job description. To begin, ask yourself:

What do I need from a Listener?
What do I need from an Enforcer?

There are different kinds of Enforcers, and each of us may need something different. In my case, I'm a very thick-skinned person: my feelings aren't easily hurt, and I'm not easily intimidated, so I don't easily back down. Therefore, I don't need an Enforcer who simply tells me the truth. Instead, I need somebody who's going to risk shaking me up by saying, "Listen! This is really important and the time is now!" because some people may tell you the truth, but they do it passively, and that is not an Enforcer, that's just a truth teller.

You should always be evaluating the effectiveness of your team members—in a very nonjudgmental way. There'll be times when you have to face that this is not the team member that you need in your life at this moment, but that doesn't mean they're a bad person.

You Need Friends, Not Fans, on Your Team

Fans will cheer you on even when you do the wrong thing. But friends will hold you accountable for what it is that you haven't done well. In essence, fans will cheer you on to your death. But friends will give you real tough love so you don't ever have to fail. I realized very early in my broadcast career that I wanted friends around me and not fans. If I was ever to get to the next level, it wasn't going to be because of the people who cheered for me, but because of the people who supported me.

At the end of the day, the people in our circle allow us to stand on their shoulders and use our own strength to reach the next level. That's the opposite of the people who allow us to lean against them to avoid falling down.

When I told my friend Paul, "I don't need you to be a fan, I need you to be a friend," that was me evaluating his response to the job description that I had placed out there for "Friend." The friend that I needed him to be maybe was the Enforcer, maybe the Rock, and maybe the Soldier. More than likely, at that point in my life, it was the Soldier. I needed somebody who was going to roll with me. You don't typically see Soldiers congratulating each other every time they complete a task. That's what I needed Paul to do for me at that time in my life, on my journey.

As I said, Paul was taken aback by my statement, but not by the sentiment. When I explained to him that I wasn't being an egomaniac when I said, "I've got enough fans, I don't need another one," what I meant was that he was in my inner circle because I valued who he was and his opinions. His access to me gave him a critical look at who I really am. What I needed was more than a celebration of my accomplishments. I needed a critical voice, someone who would give me advice that the average person who watches me on television could never give. Paul's reaction was great: he really appreciated my frankness, and what started as a very blunt conversation ended up with a very positive outcome that actually improved our relationship.

In fact, at the beginning of each year, I usually have conversations with the people in my life to ask them what they need from me as a friend, and to tell them what I need from them. I tell them about some of the things that I've got going on and where I'm trying to take my life, and we talk about how we can help one another.

Sometimes in life, we expect everything to happen organically, but things do not happen that way. Things happen because you diligently plan and strategize for them to be that way. Sometimes we expect the people in our lives to be mind readers but we've never told them what we need. Whether you've evolved and want something new or changed direction, if your friends or the people in your circle aren't briefed, then you shouldn't assume they can figure it out on their own. That's not playing fair. Tell people what you need from them!

Remember, you may have this conversation with a close friend, and that person may respond by saying, "I don't think I can do that, man," or "I'm not comfortable doing that, because you're such a strong person, it would intimidate me." Don't be put off by that type of response, because at least now you know what you can expect from that person.

Job Descriptions

When you're selecting your team members, let each person know the "job description." They have to know what you need. What's the required skill set for being a successful Listener, or an effective Enforcer? You also need to let your team members know, "This is what I need to accomplish, and I really would appreciate it if, this year, maybe once a month, you'd tell me where I am in relation to this particular objective."

I've counseled many young men on how to become a better mate. Becoming a better mate is not about being perfect; it's about changing your expectation of what you find acceptable. Many men want to play the field until they decide to get married. They've spent their whole lives being cheaters, and then one day they think because they like someone that they're going to be faithful when they've never practiced being faithful.

When I'm counseling young men about moving to a place where they can build healthy relationships, I tell them they need to have men around them who are dedicated to helping them do exactly that. If you want to create a healthy relationship, but your boys are always introducing you to new women even when they know you have a girlfriend, they aren't aligned with your objective. Instead, you need a team member who's confident and strong enough to say to you, "Wait a minute, man, you told me you wanted to be faithful to this girl. So what's going on over here?"

Assuming that someone can handle the role you need, based on what you know about him or her, without a direct confirmation that he or she can handle the role is a big gamble. In addition, if you take this route, you'll ultimately have to work harder because you'll constantly have to assess the situation. For this reason, I always recommend overcoming your fear and having direct conversations with the people you want on your team. After all, if you feel they should be part of helping you achieve your personal best, you should feel comfortable talking to them about it.

Suppose you have a direct conversation with someone, and you say, "Look, this is really what I need from you this year. Can you be my Enforcer when you see me slipping? Will you demand my attention when I'm not listening to reason? Will you tell me the truth when everybody else is telling me what they think I want to hear?"

If a team member doesn't fulfill their role, you have to provide them with feedback. "In January, we had a conversation, and I told you what I needed from you. I didn't say that to you because I thought it sounded good. I really need your help. You said you'd have my back but you didn't deliver. Are you serious about being able to fulfill this position? Or do I need to find somebody else to be my Enforcer?" This gives you the ability to not only have people on your team who'll hold you accountable, but you can also hold them accountable to fulfill their roles as well. To me, that's really the only fair way to do this.

On the other hand, know that the people on your team cannot make you be your best. You have to make you be your best. Your team members are there to support you, but they can't lead your life for you. If they try to, it's your choice that's blown up in your face. Your problem is that you aren't committed to your vision. Nobody can be more committed to your vision than you, because at the end of the day, if this isn't a workable model for achieving your personal best, you need to figure out one that is.

Ultimately, the journey to achieving your personal best is not anyone's responsibility except yours. This is a critical component, and it's integral to the leadership training I do, because if you're a leader, you can't get to where you want to go if you don't have a good team of people around you. The best leaders are the people who have the best teams. The best business people I see are the people who have the best teams.

President Barack Obama is an example of such a leader. We don't need to know who specifically is on his team, but it's obvious that President Obama did not organize his Facebook campaign; somebody else did that for him. He had a technical director who was able to use cell phones, Web pages, Facebook, and MySpace in a way that no candidate did previously. Somebody on his team made sure that they utilized modern technology on every level to engage people around electoral politics in a way they had never before been engaged.

President Obama also had somebody on his team who was an amazing speechwriter, somebody who knew his voice, somebody who understood his vision, and somebody who understood his desires. Obama delivered amazing speeches, but he didn't write them all. There was a speechwriter doing that.

The president also had one of the most amazing volunteer corps that we've ever seen in electoral politics. There's no way that President Obama could have been in every state, training people how to be campaigners or campaign volunteers. Instead, he had a volunteer coordinator at the national level who was training people in every one of these states so that they'd be able to train people at the local level, who'd then be able to train volunteers.

President Obama looked like the master candidate because he had a team of people that was able to do things he didn't have time to do, so he could focus on other critical tasks. As a leader, he was able to identify the people who could work at maximum capacity, not only to make his job easier; but also to help him reach his goal, which was to become president. To become president, you have to have a clear vision, and get people to buy into that vision. Obama was able to put a team together that could go to the people, could speak various languages so he could speak to different demographics, and could clearly present what the vision was, which was change.

Whether he came up with the change thing or somebody else came up with it, his team did the marketing. He didn't market it. He didn't design the logo and put it on T-shirts, or figure out all the other products the campaign put out there that people could wear or use, which made people feel part of the Obama movement. A team of people around him dealt not only with policy issues and came up with his platform, but they also got out there, serving as his street teams and volunteer chairs.

In the beginning, he was the candidate who was there by himself, and he had to pick those people who ultimately came on board to manifest it. All good leaders know how to pick the teams that can help them get to the destination. It's not just about picking a team. It's about picking the right team. President Obama's almost seamless campaign and ultimate election are an example of someone picking a team that was able to make those things happen.

Now, maybe you can't relate to my example of how then-candidate and now-President Obama chose people for his team, so consider Caroline's story.

Caroline was a graduate of the University of Wisconsin–Madison with decent grades, who returned to her hometown of Milwaukee to teach. From the moment we met, she talked about education, how important it was, and the impact it had on her. She remembered that when she was a child, reading, extracurricular activities, and school had saved her life. Her girlfriends had joined gangs, they had become pregnant early, or they just didn't finish school. For Caroline, school was a kind of sanctuary.

Despite the fact that she had recognized that she wanted to be different from her high school friends, when she returned to Milwaukee after graduating from college, she started hanging out with these same girls. Apparently, she felt some loyalty to these old friends. I think that sometimes we create our teams because of a sense of guilt or misplaced responsibility or simply out of habit. And that's what happened to Caroline: she fell into a routine of just going to work, coming home, doing her lesson plans, grading tests, then going to work, coming home, doing her lesson plans, etc. In other words, she was doing the bare minimum of life. One reason for this was that there was nobody in her life to push her to achieve her personal best.

I met her at a church where I'd preached about this whole notion of pulling people together. I'd talked about Jesus and the disciples, and that Jesus, who was God in man, still needed twelve people to help him walk out his ministry. The point obviously was, "If Jesus needed twelve people, why do you think you can do it by yourself?"

I also pointed out that Jesus didn't get twelve people who looked exactly like him. Jesus didn't get twelve people with the same skills and abilities that he had. And Jesus didn't get his home boys with whom he'd grown up to be on his team. Instead, Jesus chose people along his road in which he saw a reflection of what he needed to accomplish, what he was charged to do. That was the message of my preaching that day.

Anyway, a few years later, I was back in Milwaukee doing some work around the election, and I ran into Caroline again. She reminded me of our first encounter. She told me that "the team thing saved me." She was rolling with her girls back then, the same girls that she hung out with in high school. They weren't doing anything with their lives, and they thought the fact that she was teaching was enough, but there were all these other things that she wanted to do with her life. It was after I spoke that she started looking at the people in her circle and realized that she was never going to get to where she wanted to go if the people in her circle didn't even want to step outside their own boxes.

It was then she began to discover new people to hang out with. She befriended people who were able to support attitudes she'd never had before. She was accepted to an educational leadership master's program and claimed a limitless future.

Caroline freed herself to take responsibility for achieving her personal best. She explained to me that one of the biggest barriers to creating a new team of people when she returned to Milwaukee was that initially she felt that, by leaving her old friends off the team, she was telling them that they were bad people. After Caroline heard my talk, she recognized that wasn't what changing team members meant. It meant only that those high school friends couldn't help her get to where she wanted to go. For Caroline, that was a huge realization—one that changed the direction of her life.

Scouting

Choosing a team is almost like being a professional sport scout who hits the road in search of the top talent required for a championship team. When scouts recruit, they know what positions the kids they're scouting play, and more important, they know what positions their team needs to fill. This knowledge allows them to look at the potential team members in relation to their team's total needs.

Most of us, of course, don't receive scouting reports or go out looking for teammates. We're just living our lives, and that's okay. But you have to keep your scouting eyes open. By that, I mean that every time you meet someone, every time someone crosses your path, part of what you should be doing—and this is what I do—is ask yourself, "Why did this person cross my path? Is this somebody with whom I might be able to do business? Or is this somebody who might potentially be a friend?"

If you always have your scouting hat on, when you're introduced to somebody new, or are having a new level of conversation with someone you already know, you'll be able to get a sense of who they are and what they want, and if they merge with who you are and what you want.

This is not opportunism. It's about seeing if there is a fusion of identity and desire that makes this person a potential team member for you. And usually (although not in all cases), if somebody is on my team, I'm on his or her team, too. The roles we fill for each other may be different, and may manifest themselves differently, but seldom have I found somebody who's on my team when I'm not on theirs. That's another reason to have those update conversations each year—so you can explore how you can truly help each other. It's also why I think it's important to say, "This is what I need from you. What do you need from me?"

Before we leave this topic, it's important to emphasize again that nobody can be more dedicated to your vision than you. Therefore, if one of your team members is more dedicated to what your vision is than you are, something is wrong, and the result will be the kind of conflict that leads to a dysfunctional team. It's essential to understand that, when you build your team, you're creating a mechanism of accountability. If, for some reason, you shirk that responsibility, you're setting yourself up, not to only destroy your team, but also to destroy the relationships with your teammates.

Give All of Yourself

As a track athlete, I remember always wondering how Olympian Carl Lewis was able to win all those races right at the very end. Very seldom did he come out of the blocks faster than everyone else and rarely was he winning at the halfway point, but almost always at the eighty- or ninety-meter mark Carl Lewis would come on and finish the hundred-meter race in first place, often edging many of his competitors right at the finish line.

As I studied the science of racing, I learned that it wasn't so much that Carl Lewis was going faster at the end of the race, it was just that everyone else was slowing down faster than he was. When you're willing to give your all, consistently and passionately, everyone else will slow down faster than you will. When you don't give enough in the beginning, then there's no way you'll have enough in the end to finish—let alone win.

There's a great line in the science fiction movie *Gattaca,* starring Ethan Hawke, Uma Thurman, and Jude Law. Ethan Hawke's character, Vincent Freeman, and his brother (in a flashback) are racing each other across a lake. It's more a game than a race, a game of "swimming chicken," actually, in which the two men are supposed to swim as far as possible across the lake before turning around at the last moment and swimming back. The one who swims the farthest out, naturally, wins. When his brother asks Ethan's character how he always managed to win the race when they were boys, Ethan's character explains, "You want to know how I did it? This is how I did it...I never saved anything for the swim back."

I think of that line often when I'm slowing down at the end of another long day on the road or not exactly looking forward to yet another layover in yet another crowded airport on the way to give yet another speech.

What am I saving my energy for?
What am I waiting for?

Conventional wisdom seems to be that fame, money, and the good life can come overnight. The success of hip-hop artists proves that you can become famous from nothing but a hot ring tone. Right. Reality television proves that you can become famous with little or no talent. Wrong. The truly good life—which comes from reaching your best and possessing a sense of fulfillment—cannot happen simply because you want it. You can't pull it out of a hat; it can't happen overnight. If you want to complete this journey, you have to work for it. Hard work does still pay off, and if you give your best, you can get your best in return.

Fortunately, a work ethic is a highly transferable skill. For example, when I was a kid, I practiced running on the track when no one else was there. I charted the times that the top runners in the country had achieved that week and, in the middle of the night, I started exercising. I wanted to work out when I thought all my competition might be sleeping.

Similarly, when I was president of the Black Student Union in college, the Student Union that housed our office closed at midnight each day. I'd hide behind my desk until the security guards made their final check so I could continue working for several more hours while other students were partying or sleeping. In addition, when I started working at the national headquarters of the NAACP, I could have counted on two fingers the number of people who came in earlier or stayed later than I did. Solidly imprinted in my DNA was a good work ethic.

If you already have a solid work ethic, this chapter will guide you through the process of working smarter. Your intellect is a power that can take you places that your physical will cannot. Many people work hard every day and find themselves stuck in the same place. I want to see you work smart and change your reality.

Work ethic + intellect = the greatest returns!

If you have a weak work ethic, don't put yourself on suicide watch just yet, because this chapter will be especially helpful to you. It will help you realize where you're weak and help you create some new habits that encourage increased effort and advanced output. I'll take you through a process that will challenge you to discover what you really want. Because when you're honest about what you want, you'll discover what it takes for you to get there.

This chapter reveals the importance of consistency in achieving your goal. No longer can you give the minimum and expect the maximum in return. This chapter also covers issues like time management, sacrifice, focus, delegation, and the difference between working hard and working smart. There are no shortcuts on this road. If you don't give your best, you won't get your best.

The reason you have to put everything on the line isn't because life is unfair or you're doing penance for some bad act. You have to put everything on the line because everything you're supposed to become requires the whole you. Therefore, if you only give half of yourself, you only become half of who you're supposed to be. How amazing would it be, especially for those of you who think you're happy with what you're currently giving, who've never given all of yourself—to give it all and reap all the benefits? Think of how much you could have if you gave it your all!

When people come up to me from my hometown, it would be difficult to explain to them that I'm depressed because I'm not thinking about where I am but where I could be "if only." If only I'd prepared myself more for that speech, or pushed myself harder for that client. If only I'd called that one person whose card I left in the hotel room. If only I'd followed up on that project that I saw someone else do a year later. The things that have fallen through the cracks are what scare me the most. I'm not impressed with what I've done, I'm aware of what I've allowed to go by the wayside—the missed opportunities, the undervalued relationships and the halfhearted attempts because I failed to give my all.

The Myth of the Overnight Sensation

Our culture, driven primarily by media, has created the impression that we can get things easily that actually have to be earned. We see it on *Who Wants to Be a Millionaire.* We see it with local lottery winners. We see it in entrepreneurs no one even heard of yesterday getting multimillion-dollar business deals, or athletes getting huge sports contracts, or musicians going platinum, or first-time filmmakers selling twenty million tickets. All of these images repeated over and over again give the appearance that you, too, can make it overnight. In just thirty seconds, you could be a millionaire. In twenty seconds, you can be a superstar.

The media bears some of the blame for this "overnight" sensation phenomenon, because it's easier to tell the story of overnight success than to describe ten or twenty years of hard work required to achieve celebrity status. When you hear about a recording artist whose first album has gone platinum, you don't usually learn that he's been in the business—or trying to get into the business—for years.

I was at a conference sponsored by Congressman Elijah Cummings with writer, actor, and recording artist Ne-Yo, who is an accomplished songwriter. He's written for everybody from Mariah Carey to Céline Dion, and he recently gained a great deal of fame for his solo singing career. Speaking to a group of young people, he was asked how it felt to be on top of the industry. His answer makes my point: "I don't think you get it. I was doing this for *twelve years* before anybody knew who I was." Nobody knew that because the media doesn't talk about the long hours or the lonely nights. Instead, they make it seem that yesterday you never heard of him, today he's a superstar.

For twelve years Ne-Yo was writing *every single day.* He took stories from everyday life, and in every spare moment he wrote song lyrics, created poems, told stories through his music when no one was paying attention. He just realized that he had to perfect his craft to be taken seriously. Because it's not glamorous to read all about the sweat and hard work, the spin causes many of us to believe that the work ethic is unimportant. At the end of the day, it's a solid work ethic that enabled these "overnight sensations" to succeed.

Similarly, Jay-Z, hip-hop artist and business tycoon, tells a great story about always having a pen and paper with him wherever he went. He was *constantly* writing and memorizing his material, no matter what else he was doing. According to him, the further he physically went from the Marcy Projects in Brooklyn, the more he wrote and memorized. Taking the train he might memorize eight bars, or another sixteen bars. Eventually, he was able to memorize a whole song during a train ride. But as he left the city on trains, taking him from New York to D.C. or New York to Virginia, he did more than write and memorize. It was his conscious life experience that made him a great MC.

Hard Work Does Pay Off

Too many people believe that no matter how hard they work, they won't be successful. You can't give in to that belief, though, because there are just as many times that it's a misconception. Remember, you've already admitted that there is something great out there for you. So you have to also believe that on the other side of the journey is that success. Hard work is what exists in the middle of where you are and where you want to be. Hard work often does pay off, and here is just one example:

Alisha grew up in Florida in the Miami area, in an average working class household, without a whole lot of money, but she was encouraged at an early age to adopt a strong work ethic. At Spellman College in Atlanta, Alisha was the college chapter president of the NAACP. She had a real passion to make a difference, and decided she wanted to run for office right out of college. I found it interesting that this was one of her goals, because she'd just run for election inside the NAACP for a youth board seat in a quite contentious election. She was very aggressive about getting her message out to the youth in her region and letting people know that she was serious. Unfortunately, despite her hard work, she lost that NAACP race.

Because she lost, some people discouraged her intention to run for public office. They wanted to know what made her think she could run for a state legislator's seat in the State of Georgia. She'd be running against a person twenty-plus years older who'd held the seat for four terms, in a predominantly white district, and she was a young black woman who couldn't win a youth race inside an organization that she'd been a part of since childhood. Alisha didn't listen to these naysayers. She realized that nobody was going to work harder than she was.

I have to admit that even I was a little skeptical—and I knew how hard Alisha could work! Therefore, I cautioned her that work ethic is one thing, but common sense is another, because I really believed that the odds were against her to win. I didn't want to see a young leader damaged forever by two losses within a very short period of time. I wanted her to be realistic about her ambitions, and agreed to support her in any way I could. Her steadfast response was that I should trust her because her work ethic and what she was willing to put into this was above and beyond what anybody else was willing to do. There was nothing I could do to dissuade her from running. Even against the odds, I knew it was a wait-and-see-what-happens election.

As a political scientist, I know that most young people who run for office don't usually win their first time out. Instead, they often have a rough showing, they get their name out there, they gain credibility, and they put themselves in the position to be able to win their second or third time out. Yet Alisha was focused on winning, beating the streets like nobody I've ever seen before, going door to door—because she knew that, in a district where she was running against an incumbent, she wouldn't have a chance to win if people heard her name only once. She made certain that voters not only saw who she was and knew who she was, but also that they knew they could trust her ability to represent them.

She participated in every debate—and was prepared. She studied the issues inside and out, and knew them cold. And she did it: she beat the incumbent! It was an incredibly close race—she won it by only 4 or 5 percent—but it doesn't matter how close it is; it only matters who wins. She was a first-time candidate, but Alisha Thomas Morgan won that election, and she's still a sitting representative. Her success was the result of determination and hard work. She gave all of herself.

Will Smith made an unusual statement regarding his success due to his work ethic over all else. He has been quoted on *60 Minutes* saying, "I've never really viewed myself as particularly talented. I've viewed myself as slightly above average in talent. Where I excel, though, is a ridiculous, sickening, work ethic. You know, while the other guy is sleeping, I'm working. While the other guy is eating, I'm working." He even joked and said, "While the other guy is making love, I'm making love, too, but I'm working really hard at it." He is very clear that, for him, the work ethic is what made him successful and it's the cornerstone of who he is.

Work ethic comes from several sources. One is hunger: the desire for something you don't have. You'll hear someone say something like, "I want this more than I want anything else. I know that if I don't scratch, crawl, and climb to have it, I'm not going to get it." I have a mentee named John. I met John from either an experience that was divine or the most productive accident I know of. I was meeting a friend of mine, Jamie Hector from HBO's *The Wire,* so that he could introduce me to two boys who were part of an organization he started that mentored kids. They were interested in television production, and wanted to potentially be interns on the second season of *The Truth with Jeff Johnson.* As I was talking to them, Jamie noticed John, a young man who worked at the Cosi restaurant in Manhattan where we were meeting. John was listening to our conversation from across the room. He'd already made an impression on Jamie, who told me later that John had some of the best customer service skills he'd even seen. With that as the first impression, Jamie invited John to the table to sit with us.

I realized after the first two questions that John was a bright young man who needed to be pushed. I asked him what he wanted to do with his life, what he wanted to be, and how he planned to do it. He talked about his desire to get into a physical therapy program and perhaps even to play football in college. Most of all, he said he wanted to do something different, something meaningful. I asked him why he wasn't already in college or working another plan, and after giving me every good excuse, he gave me several bad ones. I told him that I'd help him get into any school he wanted to go to if he would (a) read *The Alchemist* by Paulo Coelho; (b) fill out the application for the school(s) he was interested in; and (c) research the specific academic programs that he could see majoring in. Within one week, John had done all of them.

John continued to push himself to talk to the people that I connected him with at the college I attended, the University of Toledo. He studied for the ACT and kept his job to put some money away for school. He stayed at work because he wanted to change his life from what it was to what it could be. Several months later the University of Toledo accepted him, where today he is working on his undergraduate degree. While it was just one phase of his journey, it was his work ethic that allowed him to give his all and claim his best.

There's another type of work ethic, which is learned. I work the way I saw my father work. My parents divorced when I was eight years old, and at the time, my dad was involved in an entrepreneurial venture with his brother-in-law at a junkyard. He had always had an entrepreneurial spirit, and here was an opportunity to make money in a business my uncle was already in. At some point, though, my dad realized that it was not what he wanted to do, and he decided to go the corporate route and got a job in human resources.

My parents had joint custody of my brother and me. When we were with my dad, he got us up in the morning and made sure we were ready for school. We left for school, and he went to work. After school, we had to call him, because he wanted to be certain we were home. Then when he came home, he cooked dinner, checked our homework, and then left for his graduate school classes at night. At the same time, he was working a full-time job and taking care of us (we were in middle school and high school by this time, so he could leave us alone in the evenings), and was also taking night classes to get his MBA. When he got home from his classes, he did his own homework. The next morning, that brutal schedule started all over again.

Meanwhile, I was watching. I saw him working this way, and even when I was young, I must have imitated it because my mother (who—let's keep this story straight—worked hard as well) has often said to me, "You work the way your father works." So, I believe my work ethic, from a business standpoint, comes from my father's example.

Even before I saw how hard my father worked, though, I'd already developed a strong work ethic as an athlete, which came from always wanting to be the best. I didn't want to lose; I didn't want anybody to beat me; I wanted to be the best on the track all the time. And I knew there was no way I could do that if I didn't constantly work harder than the next person.

There's both an innate hunger that comes from wanting to be the best at what you do and a learned work ethic that comes from watching the people around you, your parents, friends, and even acquaintances and historical role models. Darryl, a kid I know, told me he read Russell Simmons's, *Do You!: 12 Laws to Access the Power in You to Achieve Happiness and Success,* memoir in the seventh or eighth grade. Darryl was from the inner city. He didn't know who his father was, and his mother didn't have very much, but Darryl was determined to have his own business. He didn't even know the kind of business he was going to own, he just knew he was going to have his own business. Russell Simmons's book *Do You!* helped Darryl develop his work ethic. Simmons wrote about working twenty to twenty-two hours a day, trying to build the Def Jam record label, and that dedication was Darryl's motivation. He didn't know Russell Simmons, had never met Russell Simmons. No one in Darryl's house or his circle worked as hard as Russell described. But all it took to inspire Darryl was a vision of someone else's work ethic and an understanding of the manifestation of that work ethic—which was Def Jam and the rest of the Russell empire—for Darryl to say to himself, "If this worked for him, why can't it work for me?"

Your Work Ethic Needs to Match Your Desire

When I talk about work ethic in my seminars, usually I connect it to the idea of how badly you want something. So the first question I ask is, "Is your work ethic consistent with your desires?" I ask this question because I often find that people want things, but they're not willing to work for them.

There are people who claim they want to graduate from high school, but then they cut class. There are people who say they want a promotion, but they don't keep up with what's going on in their field, and they don't study new trends that would make their knowledge base worthy of a promotion. There are people who claim they want to become entrepreneurs, but they still want to work from nine to five—and it doesn't matter what business you're in, you can't be an entrepreneur and only work from nine until five—starting and growing a business just doesn't work that way.

Therefore, the first place to start is by answering the question I posed above: "Is my work ethic consistent with what I say I want?"

If your answer is no, then you have to go back to the earlier question, from Chapter 4: "What is my vision?"

If you still have that desire, that original vision for something you want, then you almost have to reprogram yourself, because the work that you'll have to put out to get there may be greater than what you've been willing to give. Only then can you start dealing with the practical issues related to achieving your goal, which pertain to training yourself to improve your work ethic. As a track athlete, when I was training for the 200-meter sprint, I knew from the time the gun went off that I needed to be running as hard as I could. Therefore, to prepare, I ran repeat 350-meter sprints during practice because I knew that most of my competition was preparing themselves for the 200 by practicing the 200. But if I trained myself to run as hard as I could for 300 or even 350 meters, then, when I was actually in the 200-meter race, I knew that I could sprint the whole race strong. I wouldn't slow down at the 200-meter mark because I'd trained myself to run past that mark. And that would enable me to win the race.

So, I trained for 300s or 350s instead of 200s. That put my body—my legs, my lungs, my mind—in a place where, although I knew I was going to be competing in the 200, I was prepared to sprint 350. You have to do the same thing when you prepare yourself to strengthen your work ethic, to achieve what you ultimately want to do. You need to push yourself even farther, even harder than where you really want to go, to ensure that you won't fall short, you won't give up, and you'll attain the goal you've set for yourself.

How to Work Smarter

Now, you may be thinking my example of running 350 meters to prepare for a 200-meter race doesn't really apply to improving your work ethic in other areas of your life. After all, there are only twenty-four hours in a day, so you can't think you're going to train yourself to work twenty-four hours straight to get the most out of sixteen hours. However, your work ethic involves more than putting in extra time: it's about training yourself to use the time you have in the most effective way possible. You may spend too much time on the Internet, or watching TV, or just daydreaming—time that you could be using more productively. So, it isn't about creating three hours in the day that don't exist. It's about using the twenty-four hours you have more effectively. When you develop your work ethic to use the hours you have more effectively, you're consciously deciding how best to focus and spend your time.

Let's say you're trying to improve your work ethic in your business. You have to let go of, and sacrifice, certain other things that you do so you can focus more time on your business. You have to determine which things you can spend less time on. You can start by asking yourself, "Where is the thirty minutes to an hour that I can shift from doing something else over to my business?" By doing that, you're no longer treating your business as if it's a nine-to-five job; instead, you're treating it like the entrepreneurial venture it is, and giving it the focus needed to make it successful.

Sometimes people say they're doing so much that they cannot possibly give any more. I don't buy that. My dad understood that he was working a nine-to-five job, taking care of his kids, and going to class and studying for his master's degree. He also knew he had to make dinner for us, so he became a master at preparing Crock-Pot dinners: he was the Crock-Pot king. He realized that using the Crock-Pot was a way for him to spend less time actually cooking dinner because the dinner was cooking itself all day while he was at work, and we still had great food. Don't sleep on the Crock-Pot meals. We had beef ribs that would melt off the bones and chili that could win a prize. The Crock-Pot was also a way to keep him from being completely worn out. Dad used it on days when he had night classes and recognized that every moment of his day would be busy. Part of a healthy work ethic is about finding ways to work smarter. It's not all about working harder, just working hard and smart.

There are times when you're going to be exhausted, you're going to feel worn out, and there's nobody in the world who reaches his or her personal best without that. Many of us want things, but we don't ever want to hurt to get them. Whether you're an athlete doing the reps until it burns, or a writer writing until you must lay your head down before you bang it on the computer, or perhaps executives deciding at 2 AM that they need to go home or their spouses aren't going to let them sleep there anymore, you have to push the limits of what's normally comfortable for you. Being your best is not about being average. First, I tell people that you're going to stretch yourself and it's going to hurt. Unfortunately, too often, we stretch ourselves for mediocrity instead of our best. We put in a fair number of hours doing things, but what we're doing it for and how we're doing it isn't taking us to our best, it's merely keeping us in the cycle we're already in. So the question to ask yourself is, "How do I shift this work ethic to focus it on the things that are going to get me to my best, instead of on the things that have me running around in circles in a place that I don't want to be?"

Those who want to be their best are the ones who are willing to focus their time, energy, effort, creativity, and thought to achieve all they need to get it done. Those who with a merely good work ethic are working hard, but often lack the focus required to accomplish the true task at hand. Therefore:

Work ethic + focus = greater power!

Often people work hard, but they spread themselves too thin when they should be focusing their work in one place that helps get them to their best. At the beginning of every day, I think it's important to ask yourself:

What do I have to get done today that will take me toward my personal best?

If that's the first question, then everything else you do you must weigh against your answer. If, instead, as people often do, you start the day saying, "This is what I want," you're off in fifteen different directions before the day has begun. You're working hard, but you're all over the place. That's why it's important to focus on what you have to accomplish today to get there, instead of focusing on just the things you want.

Once you've answered the first question, then you should ask yourself:

What don't I have to get accomplished today?

And you'll know exactly where you are and what you have to do. It seems like a crazy question, but it can actually be quite empowering.

One of the things I watch people do—and I'm guilty of it myself sometimes—is convince themselves that they must get things done that day that they actually don't. They may run around trying to accomplish something they told themselves needed doing that day, when in fact it could have waited until the weekend. You need to determine what task is most important to you. Is completing your business plan more important than doing your spring cleaning today? Once you get your business plan done, you're setting yourself up to actually operate the business, and your house is not going to fall apart if it's dirtier than you'd like for another week. You might be uncomfortable, but once you get the business plan done, you can go back to cleaning.

If you choose spring cleaning, you're postponing things you need to do to reach your personal best to deal with daily maintenance that could actually wait. One of my favorite lines from the Denzel Washington and Forest Whitaker movie *The Great Debaters* is when Whitaker's character is standing opposite his very excited fourteen-year-old, college freshman son. His son has just burst into his father's office to tell him how excited he is about the debate team. His father, a professor at the college, asks in the calmest of voices, "What do we do?" His son on cue answers, "We do what we have to do so that we can do what we want to." That is exactly what we do when we focus our work.

Donald and I went to middle school and high school together. He and I weren't close friends, but we were cool. He was one of those people I didn't keep in touch with, but I saw him at my ten-year reunion. We were talking, and I asked him what he was doing. He told me he was a bail bondsman. It turned out he owned about five or six locations in different parts of the state.

I was surprised because this is an unusual career choice: personally, I don't wake up each day thinking that if this journalism thing goes bad, I can become a bail bondsman. No offense intended, I asked him what made him become a bail bondsman.

He told me it was a easy choice because he was getting locked up over and over again for stupid stuff—he never said what that "stupid stuff" was—and he got tired of it. So he decided he had to change his life, he needed to start working harder, and he needed to make sure he had a future. Thinking about what was around him, he realized that every time he got locked up, someone was running to a bail bondsman to get him out. "What struck me was that when everything else was closed, the bail bondsman was open. Here is a twenty-four-hour-a-day, seven-day-a-week business. People are always going to jail, so people always need to get out. If I had spent as much time helping people get their friends out of jail as I spent going to jail, I wouldn't have been in this situation in the first place. I already knew the other side of it, which was going to jail. All I needed to do was create the business model to get people out of jail. Then, I just started busting my ass. I opened up one place, and it went well, and I was able to open another location, and that was it."

In other words, Donald's work ethic shifted 180 degrees because he was tired of being where he was. It also demonstrates that role models can come from anywhere. In a way, Donald was his own role model, because he did the opposite of what he'd been doing.

The same is true of your work ethic, which, if properly focused, can turn your life around. Donald didn't go to school or take some courses to do this. He simply decided to turn his life around, and with the same effort, perhaps using the same work ethic that got him into jail, he built a business.

How Does Your Work Ethic Rate?

The term *work ethic* is often used, but it's rare that we actually gauge and rate our work ethic.

If you're going to be honest with yourself about the work ethic that you're putting into achieving your personal best, you have to look at it as if you were the professor on the outside who has to grade how you're doing. What grade would you give yourself and why? For instance, you might give yourself a C and say, "Needs to give more. Is giving at a middling level, but still has more to give," or an F, "Doesn't try at all," or a B, "He gives a great deal, but is not strategic."

Based on the things that we've talked about in this chapter, how would you rank yourself and why? Once you do this, you'll have a personal understanding of the parts of your work ethic that need improvement. Along the way, it's important to assess each aspect of your life and how hard you're working toward each goal. Now, we're looking at the whole picture, your overall work ethic that reflects how hard you work toward your personal best.

How would you rate what you give, sacrifice, and put on the table for that vision that you stated was the place you wanted to go?

Sometimes people tell me they're working hard toward some of their goals, but they can't work hard toward all of the goals. My first response is, they have to tell me what they mean by *can't* because when you say you can't it implies that there are forces outside your control that are preventing you from giving all you have. That's bull.

Others may say, "I'm working hard in some areas, but not working as hard in other areas." My response is, That's why you need to grade your work ethic. In what areas are you weak, and why? Making this assessment, you're then able to determine what you need and how to obtain it. What you really need is a new perspective. Working hard in one area and not another is often about your perspective. If you have the ability to give your all on one thing, you have the ability to put the same amount of effort on the table for all things. The question is, will you?

PART III

STRATEGIZE, STREAMLINE, AND SACRIFICE

Strategize: Plan for Your Best

Your strategy is the most pragmatic step on your journey to becoming your personal best. In this chapter, we'll examine how to determine the road you take to get from where you are today to your destination, which is that vision you created in Chapter 4: the daily, weekly, and monthly habits and processes you'll incorporate into your daily living that actually transform your life. This is a difficult step, because there's no room for an unclear conceptualization, ambiguity, or vague explanation. It's here that you tell yourself what you must actually do along the road to get to your personal best.

Getting from Where You Are to Where You Want to Be

There are several parts to developing your strategy, and you'll be fusing all you learned about yourself in earlier chapters with a to-do list that'll guide you on your way. To complete this process, you'll need:

- *A journey map:* This is how you'll identify where you are now and where you want to be—your destination. On it, you'll plot the steps you need to take to get from one to the other.

- *A transformation calendar*: You'll use this calendar to track your daily and weekly activities. You can go old school and use a date book, or you can go high-tech and use your BlackBerry or iPhone—either one, as long as it's *always* with you.

- *Power notes:* This is your personal notebook, your journal—where you'll chronicle your progress and problems, as well as your thoughts and experiences about the process as you move forward.

Once you have the required materials, you can begin the process of developing your strategy. Here's how this process can work for you.

The Journey

This is the portion of your journey map where you identify where you are spiritually, professionally, personally, and in all other aspects of your life. Although you may simply identify the areas you want to focus on when you fill in the map, it's essential that you go into detail about where you are in each part of your life in your journal. Think of the map as the picture and the journal notes as the captions. The more detailed and descriptive you are about where you are, the better you'll be about describing where you ultimately want to be.

Where Do You Want to Be? What Is Your Vision for Your Personal Best?

Take the vision you created in Chapter 4 and make any modifications or clarifications before you insert it onto the journey map. Again, you can simply identify your areas of focus on the map, but it helps the process if you include details in your notes about where you want to be and how you want to feel. I cannot stress this enough as every step you take will help you arrive at this destination, so the trip is worth the work.

Divide Your Growth Areas

In Chapter 3 we emphasized the importance of being a whole person. Here it's important to deal with each area of your life separately for the purpose of developing and targeting daily action. It may take more work to become the father you want to be than to establish the spiritual relationship you long for. Dividing your life into components now doesn't mean you're looking at yourself as a fragmented person; instead, doing so allows you to tackle each growth area strategically to maximize your personal best in each area. It's like working out. You know you want your entire body in shape, but God knows that those arms need a little more work than your legs. Those abs...we won't even talk about them. So you target your weekly workout. Each of us has different areas to work on, so don't get caught up in the number of areas. Just make sure that you've identified all the parts that make you. . .you.

Devise Your Tactics and Schedule Your Evaluations

Suppose where you are is the sick you, and where you want to be is a healthy you, and your tactics are the treatment. What will you do to get from one place to the next in each growth area? For example, you might consider this situation in the following way:

Growth Area: *Parent—spend more quality time with the kids*

Tactics:

- "I'll identify one day a month when I put the cell phone and computer away, and spend time with my kids."
- "I'll spend one hour a day, two days a week, reading to my children, helping with homework, and putting them to bed."
- "Once a week, I'll leave my kids a note telling them they're great."

Evaluating Your Progress on the Journey

Once a week, take some time to evaluate your tactics. Once a week may seem too often to some of you, but it ensures that you're moving in the right direction and gives you the opportunity to modify tactics that don't work. Here are a few ways to check your progress.

Develop Your Transformation Calendar

Plug your tactics and scheduled evaluation moments into your calendar. Then place that calendar both in a place in your house where you know you're going to look at it and in one of those devices you have that normally steals time versus saves it, so you can have it with you all the time.

Create Your Power Notes

How often you write is up to you. I recommend writing once a day to make sure your thoughts are regular and clear. For some readers, this may not be realistic, but I know many of you use Facebook, Twitter, and Skype more than once a day, so at minimum you should attempt to write three days a week.

Your entries should chronicle not only what you did and the outcome; they also should indicate how you feel about not only the outcome, but also about what you did. You have to do this because too often we only focus on getting to a destination. How you feel is equally important because this is a direct reflection on how much you really want to be there. This will help you process the change you go through on your road to your best. This will be your story.

Contact Your Team

This is important. Too often, we embark on a journey to make change, and no one in our life knows anything about it. Some readers may say, "So what? Why does anyone else have to know?" The point here is that when you let someone know what you're trying to accomplish, you immediately increase your level of accountability. Moreover, it's important that you talk to your team specifically about your goals and tactics. This will ensure that someone is pushing you, encouraging you, and helping you gauge your progress. It makes no sense to have a team and not use it.

The strategy you develop must be an honest reflection of what you are, where you are, what you want, and what specifically you'll do to get it. If you fail to be honest about one aspect of this process, you risk not maximizing your efforts and falling short of your personal best.

My Own Personal Journey Map

The journey map is not something I developed to use for formal training purposes. It's something I realized I needed for my own personal and professional purposes, and it has evolved over time.

Where I Was in 2003

I developed my first personal journey map in 2003. I'd been working at the NAACP since 1999, and I was getting my behind beat over some internal political issues. Some older staff members might have felt threatened by me because I was traveling all over the country and getting a decent amount of press. I'd been hired to increase the membership and visibility of the NAACP's Youth and College Division, which our team did. In addition, our job was to ensure that the various units in the division were compliant, both financially and programmatically, as well as trained and energized. Now, two of my bosses were telling me that I was traveling too much.

When I heard that, I thought, "Isn't that what you hired me to do?" You certainly can't do that by sitting in the office. By traveling, I was providing support to my regional field directors, the people who at that time were with these units, day in and day out. I wanted to make certain they had what they needed and that we were building partnerships in the entertainment, business, and nonprofit sectors. I also wanted the troops to see me because that helped energize them. Moreover, I had a great assistant director and unit directors who were able to deal with day-to-day operations, so there were no deficiencies in my department that anybody could highlight. I'd received no negative performance evaluations and in fact received a raise. I was a little pissed off, and realized that I had to get out of this. It was time for me to go. I think I'd done everything I could there. Let someone else come in and provide new vision and energy into this movement.

That was where I was in 2003. I'd spent approximately seven years working my way up to a senior staff position in the largest civil rights organization in the country, and was trying to figure out what was next for me. That's when I pulled out a piece of paper and drew a circle that said, "My universe." At one point on the perimeter of the circle, I wrote, "Here I am," and at the exact opposite point, I wrote, "Where I want to be." Then, I began to list where I was:

- "I am a senior staff member in this highly regarded organization."
- "I travel around the country, speaking on many college campuses."
- "I do national press at least once a month."
- "I'm making a little over a six-figure income."
- "And I'm about to turn thirty years old."

All of that was good, but I still didn't know where I wanted to go next. I didn't have a job lined up, but I knew I wanted to work for myself. That led me to write down where I wanted to be:

- "Business owner"
- "Entrepreneur"
- "Consultant"

Then, I began to narrow the focus:

- "I want to consult on leadership development."
- "I want to consult on nonprofit capacity building."
- "I want to be involved in speech coaching."

Those were the three areas where I knew I had the required skill set and core competencies that were of value to a demographic in that marketplace. I could use that as the first step toward starting my new business. That was the beginning of my journey map—identifying the starting place and the finishing point.

What Road to Take?

The next step was to evaluate my options, what roads I might take. Because I knew I did not want to stay at the NAACP anymore, I could have applied for another full-time position as executive director, national organizer, or some other senior-level position in another nonprofit organization. That was Option #1. Option #2 was to stay at the NAACP, but prepare to start my own business. Option #3 was to fly by the seat of my pants, leave the NAACP, and find something else.

For me, life is a chess game. The strategy might be to take three steps, but within each step, there are different potential moves. At that point, I didn't go any further than Step 1 and its options. I thought, "These are three first steps, and I'm just going to jump out there and roll with one of them." I did not strategize or plan it all the way out—and I ended up suffering greatly because of it.

As it turned out, I left the NAACP prematurely, without having the next step firmly in my mind. I'd gone to New York and talked to Terrie Williams about moving there to help her with her Stay Strong Foundation. She let me know that she didn't have a huge budget, and I'd have to raise my own salary. I was up to that challenge, so I left the NAACP, without having another job, with no benefits outside of COBRA, and essentially started commuting to New York, staying in the city with Gary Foster, a very good friend of mine who worked for Russell Simmons, and trying to help Terrie Williams expand her foundation.

In short, I jumped without a safety net. I was separated from my wife, but still had financial responsibilities for my wife and children. I turned thirty years old in New York City without a clue of what was next, and represented an example of what *not* to do.

That's why the journey map is so important. A journey map is about knowing more than where your first stop is going to be. The whole point of a map is to plot out where you are and *how* you're going to get where you're going. So many of us think we know where we want to end up, but can't for the life of us talk about how we plan to get there. These routes may change, but you still need the map. For instance, if I decide to drive from Washington, D.C., to Los Angeles, I may start out going into Pennsylvania and through Ohio. But I might also change my mind because of weather or some other reason and drive south into Tennessee, or Mississippi, or Alabama, and then head west across the country. But before I leave, I still need to know what roads I can travel.

At age twenty-nine I only knew where the starting point of my journey was. I hadn't plotted out alternate routes. I learned from that mistake that the journey map isn't only about my starting point. It's also about Steps 2, 3, 4, and 5, and the final steps toward my best. Plotting the course that you're going to take from beginning to end, knowing that there may be detours and roadblocks or unexpected stops and gridlock, is imperative for success. You have the benefit of my mistakes, so at least your road is mapped out. *Right!?!*

Unfortunately, I didn't do that when I left the NAACP, and suffered a great deal of financial stress. More than anything else, I learned that I couldn't navigate my life successfully without a journey map. I was never going to be stuck on the road again not knowing where to go next, or worse, having nowhere to go.

NYC Without a Journey Map

It took me about two months to come to this realization. I found myself walking one hundred blocks from 42nd Street and Broadway at Times Square, where the Stay Strong office was, up to 138th and Broadway in Harlem, where I was staying. At the time I had only $2 in my pocket, and I had to choose between taking the subway and being hungry, or walking and having something to eat when I got to Harlem. That's when I began to plan on another level.

Still, the real impetus for this new and expanded planning strategy happened when someone I'd met while at the NAACP called me and told me he was organizing a youth summit in New Haven, Connecticut, and wanted to know if I'd be willing to speak. Immediately, my journey map appeared in my subconscious. I asked him about the youth summit, and he told me his group wanted to talk to high school kids about violence, choices, employment, and other issues. I asked what the youth conference was going to look like, and he admitted he didn't really know yet. Still, I was excited about this prospect, so I told him I'd speak at the conference at no charge if he hired me as a consultant to help plan the event.

He checked with his group, they agreed, and I went to New Haven. I now had some monthly income, and used that as an opportunity to start plotting my next step. Sometimes it is the smallest opportunity that can be navigated into the largest return.

This was 2003. The election was coming up, which meant more work for people in my business. I started making a list of people I planned to contact, who might connect me with jobs when the election cycle really got into full swing. It included people I'd known from the NAACP. At the same time, I was working with this group in New Haven, which I was able to use as a springboard for a broader consulting job relating to youth and pastor outreach for another nonprofit in New Haven.

Although I wasn't able to get the work I needed in New York, I was able to take the hour-long train ride from New York City to New Haven, two to three times a week. That put some money in my pocket and fire in my belly to up my game. At the same time, I reached out to my former pastor in Baltimore, and told him I thought I was going to make another attempt at saving my marriage. I decided to move back to Baltimore and wanted to know if he had something at the church I could do. He brought me on as a full-time youth pastor.

Those steps on my journey worked out well. My consulting contract was up in Connecticut, so I was able to make the transition from New York and Connecticut back to Baltimore. The youth pastor position provided me with some health insurance and a small salary. I was closer to D.C., which allowed me to maneuver myself into a position to do the campaign work I wanted to do for the 2004 election. The strategy that I had not worked out at the beginning of 2003 was coming together at the end of the same year.

A Turning Point

Then, so many different things happened. In October of 2003, BET asked me to come on board. It happened almost accidentally. I was in Russell Simmons's office talking to some friends—not even to Russell—and having lunch. One of those friends, Alexis McGill, said she'd just had lunch with Stephen Hill, an executive at BET. She told me that they were talking about political stuff, my name came up, and he's a fan of mine. "You should give him a call," she said.

I didn't really expect much as I had no thought or desire to be on TV at the time, but I figured, times were tight and perhaps he was somebody who could take me out for a free business lunch. I mean, I had *no* desire to be on TV, I wasn't even thinking about commentary or journalism, and definitely wasn't thinking about BET—at that time, it didn't have any kind of focus on political activism. It was still mostly music, movies, and the nightly news, but that wasn't what I was looking to do. My mind hadn't gone in that direction.

Nevertheless, I e-mailed Stephen and said that Alexis had told me my name came up, and we made a date to meet for lunch. I went to his office about a week later, and the first thing he said when I walked into his office was, "Hey...Do you want to be on TV?" He didn't say hello. He didn't say, "How have you been?" Instead, he opened with, "Hey, Jeff, do you want to be on TV?" I told him I didn't really know, and I asked him what he had in mind. He told me, "I like your energy. I think you'd be good for our demographic. I want to put you on *106 & Park* or *Rap City*, but I don't know how to do it."

I suggested that I could come on *Rap City* once a week, talk about an issue, and bounce. He said, "I like it. We'll start taping next week." That was how I got started on BET, and taping began in October 2003. It wasn't really a job, because they were experimenting with me. Moreover, in a way, I was paying to be on the air, because although they paid me...well, let's just say that I was forking over twenty dollars after paying for a round-trip train ticket to get up to New York City. But it was great exposure, and you can't buy that much exposure for 20 bucks. So it was definitely worth it. I did that for a year, and then was able to finagle them into covering my travel, so at least I was now getting paid versus paying to be on TV.

At the same time, I was trying to get some real work around the upcoming election. One of the names on the list I'd put together was Donna Brazile; our paths had crossed while I was at the NAACP. But that did not mean that she'd help me find a position. I knew that part of my plan had to include contacting targeted people I'd worked with or around while at the NAACP. I called Donna, and she really was a lifesaver. I don't know if she knows how much she did for me at that time by simply making one phone call on my behalf. In the political world of the Democratic Party, when Donna Brazile makes a phone call, it's hard for the person on the other end to say no. Through her, I was able to get a position at 21st Century Democrats at the beginning of the election cycle in 2004, which opened doors to several other opportunities before the cycle was over.

So all of this—the BET work and the political work—was happening simultaneously, and it was all because I fell flat on my face after leaving the NAACP. That forced me to map out all these roads that would take me to places where I could find people who were doing the kind of work I wanted to do, and who could recommend me for positions. I was hunting for new consulting opportunities. None of that would have happened had I not first fallen on my face after leaving the NAACP and became dedicated to creating a strategy.

There Are Multiple Roads to Every Destination

Before creating your journey map, look at a real map. For example, I live in Washington, D.C., and anybody who drives in Washington, D.C., knows that there are three or four ways to get everywhere. If 295 is blocked off, you can get off on Pennsylvania Avenue and cut over to another highway. If the Baltimore-Washington Parkway is heavy, you can stay on the Beltway and go up to 95N. There is always more than one way to get anywhere. This is important because, as you create your journey map, in addition to the preferred path you want to take, be open and strategic enough to develop alternate routes.

One of the strategic things you can do in planning your journey is to forecast and prepare for roadblocks, gridlock, detours, flat tires, and such. So when they happen, you won't be immobilized.

Unfortunately, many people don't think that way. They don't like to think about what will happen if this doesn't work out. Instead, they think that they're going to do everything they possibly can to make it work out, and if it doesn't, they'll deal with it then. The result of that—as I learned the hard way—can be that you're out of a job and don't know where to go next.

Far too often, I hear someone say, "It didn't happen, so it wasn't meant to be." Sometimes that may be true, but sometimes we didn't do everything we could have done. I'm not one of those people who say that simply because something didn't happen, it wasn't meant to be. Sometimes it didn't happen because we didn't strategize correctly.

My friend, Dana, had graduated from a well-respected HBCU, and then taught English to high school students in Spain. She loved speaking Spanish daily, almost as much as she enjoyed teaching her kids. But this was a temporary post and she found herself back in the States, trying to figure out what she wanted to do next. One of the first opportunities that presented itself was a finance company, New York Life, so she accepted the job offer and started doing what you do when you're working for New York Life. She began to talk to all of the people she knew about whether they needed life insurance or death benefits, or some other financial service. She had the personality and drive for the business, so Dana was able to get a decent amount of business, but not the kind of business that was going to sustain her as a financial professional.

After Dana had been doing this for about a year, we were having lunch and it was obvious to me that she was stressed about how to keep the business moving. I asked her what she was doing and why she was trying to convince herself and the world that she wanted to be in the financial service industry. I wondered why she was pretending to herself that this is what she wanted to do. I was confused. She needed to be doing something related to Spanish, because that's what she loved. If she couldn't find a Spanish-speaking position, she should at least be working with young people. I didn't understand how Dana landed in this prison of obligation, doing what everyone expected her to do instead of what she wanted to do. She had no exit strategy to get out of this place. I knew what she wanted to do. I knew what her vision entailed. I knew that her personal best was not selling insurance. Her personal best was in changing people's lives. What was going on?

Dana agreed with my observations. She also admitted that she had no idea how to reach her professional goals. Then we began to work through the process and develop her map. Finally, Dana identified the things she'd like to do:

- "I'd like to teach in a public or private school."
- "I'd like to run my own development program for young people."
- "I'd like to work in the Foreign Service."

Those were her three starting points.

I prompted, "What do you need to do for each of these? What qualifications do you need that you don't have?" If Dana decided to teach, she could begin as a substitute teacher, but eventually would have to be certified. For the development program, she already has the qualifications needed. The Foreign Service required an application and a test. Together, we mapped out the potential skills that Dana would need for each area and talked about the potential next steps.

Dana began to take action. She interviewed for some positions. She contacted people in embassies to find out what other positions related to Foreign Service were available. She really began to follow the first few phases of this journey map that we created.

As a result, Dana is now teaching math at a Maryland public high school. She passed her certification test and developed her own nonprofit organization to engage and empower young people. She was ecstatic: I haven't seen Dana this satisfied professionally since I've known her. Dana created her map, started to follow a strategic plan, and less than six months later she was already walking in the areas she wanted to be in. Today, she is experiencing a level of fulfillment she never imagined possible.

Moreover, Dana not only began thinking about where she wanted to be professionally, but also where she wanted to be personally. In addition to the changes she made in her career, another area of her life that Dana changed was her spiritual life. She also began a different exercise routine. In addition to mapping how she was going to get to her new career goals in education, her journey map also caused her to consider such questions as: How do I find space for me to think about my road map more regularly? Dana chose prayer and meditation. She also explored how she could rejuvenate her body through yoga.

Creating her journey map was really a holistic process for Dana, and the map laid out each of those pieces. The fulfillment that Dana is experiencing right now is not just the result of her new job. It's also because she has greater peace of mind through meditation and prayer. She feels better physically because of exercise and modified eating habits, and is doing something on a daily basis that promotes and encourages a natural synergy in her life. All of these interconnected activities allow her to love what she's doing every day. When she worked for New York Life, Dana's day didn't start with prayer and meditation. She wasn't a whole person. She exercised—she went to the gym—but she was neglecting her spiritual side. Now, however, she's nurturing growth in every aspect of her life.

Create a Transformation Calendar

The transformation calendar is about accountability because so much of this program is about changing your daily behavior. It would be great if we could program ourselves simply by saying, "I'm going to change this. I'm going to do this, this, and this differently. Let me call my programmer and get my brain reprogrammed." Unfortunately, that's not how it works.

The day planner allows you to be reminded when you're going to do these things differently and what, specifically, you're going to do. Whether it's a day planner, an iPhone, or a BlackBerry, being very specific about the tasks, the objectives, the communication, and the opportunities you're going to engage in on the new road you're on helps you stay focused.

That may mean writing down that every day at 12 noon you're going to meditate; or every day, between 6:30 and 7:30 in the evening, you're going to do yoga; or at 2 PM, you'll call your wife and ask her how she's doing. Whatever it is that you're challenging yourself to do, you have to put it into a space that challenges you, on a daily basis, to do it. Otherwise, you're just leaving it to chance, where you have to force yourself to remember to do something that you haven't yet taught yourself to do.

By making your new behaviors a part of your daily planner, or putting it on your iPhone or BlackBerry, you're saying to yourself, "This is what I have to do today. This is what I'm going to do today. This is when I'm going to do it." That increases your self-accountability.

Keeping a Journey Journal

I began keeping a journey journal, my Power Notes, six years ago when I left the NAACP. My dear friend, Stephanie, was a journal fanatic. I don't know anybody who wrote more religiously than Stephanie did. It was an inspiration to me (although I've never been as consistent as she was in writing in it daily). In my seminars, I've found that men are much more resistant to keeping a journal than women are. So if you're someone who thinks that writing in a journal is only for women or metrosexual, sensitive men, don't think of it as a journal, and don't call it a journal. Instead, call it your "power notes," or anything that makes you feel gangsta enough to do it. All you need to do is log your commitments every day.

Also, many men don't realize that they already do this, they just don't do it on a personal level. I know men who constantly write Power Notes to themselves about how they're going to take over their company, or get to the next level, or achieve world domination, or even hook up with some woman. However, they often don't feel that the same thing is necessary when it's how they feel about where they are in other areas of their lives (or in life in general) and what they've done so far in their lives. However, all of these things are essential to your plan.

After all, your plan can't be about everybody else and never address the personal side of your life. If all you're doing is creating strategy about everybody else, you're neglecting the one thing that you actually have control over. You're addressing the professional side of you, but not paying attention to the whole you.

Resonating a little bit more with the brothers (and I mean brothers in the fraternity of manhood), a man's Power Notes might include: "What will help me be a better son/brother?" or a more powerful husband, or a more powerful father. If Power Notes are what men want to call this assignment, that's fine. At the end of the day, it's all about assessing where you are, what you're doing well, what you're not doing well, and then creating positive reinforcements that encourage you to reach your personal best.

Therefore, part of what this journal or these Power Notes accomplish is to chronicle your progress and your challenges in each area.

Contact Your Team

Another way to increase your level of accountability immediately is to call on your team. Let your team know where you're trying to go—for example, to be a better friend, wife, or colleague, or a better Christian, Jew, or Muslim, or a better neighbor, or whatever your vision of your personal best is—your team can support and assist you. It helps to know that you're not operating in a vacuum. In addition, if nobody knows what you're attempting, it makes it easier for you to quit or give up. Often, we'll stop or slow down the process of where we're going because it gets hard, and if nobody knows anyway, what's the big deal, right?

When I was going through this six years ago, I talked mainly to my friend Nicholle, who at that time was the Enforcer in my life (as we discussed in Chapter 6), and I spoke to her regularly. Every time I called, she asked me, "What are you doing today? Who are you talking to today? Are you out there getting that business today?" The Enforcer was the person on my team whom I talked to daily, because that was the position I most needed. I shared with her, "Here's what I want to do, and here's where I want to be."

I also spoke to my father. He wasn't the Enforcer for me, so I didn't talk to him as regularly as I talked to Nicholle. But he was and is one of the Elders on my squad, and I have always benefited from his wisdom when I listened.

Some people find it very difficult to have to check in regularly and frequently with somebody who's just going to say, "Well, why did you do *that*?" That's part of the challenge. It is not for everybody, which is why I said in the beginning that you have to share with people where you're going and what you need. The other piece that's important to remember is that when someone is truly helping you get to the place you need to be, what once may have felt tedious now feels necessary. Part of this strategy is training yourself and preparing yourself to do something that you've never done before.

Remember, when I left the NAACP, I was used to working for a large organization. I wasn't accustomed to being an entrepreneur. Although I'd worked long hours at the NAACP, the demands of being an entrepreneur were different. As an entrepreneur, I had to do everything myself, and I had to be on top of everything. So I needed someone to help me transition my personal accountability from being a hardworking employee to being an entrepreneur. For many people that's very difficult, but I had an Enforcer and an Elder who kept me accountable, and they were more essential to my progress than I could have imagined.

Use These Tools to Help You on Your Journey

The journey map, the transformation calendar, and the journey journal are tools, not burdens, and you can determine how to use them in a way that's effective for you. For some people, this is going to seem tedious and cumbersome, but others will see drastic shifts in how they spend their time and what they focus on.

For example, I'm coaching someone right now who is very unhappy with many parts of her life, but she keeps repeating the same patterns over and over and over again. In coaching Vanessa, I'm trying to develop a strategy where we don't even look at what she's doing. We first look at each area of Vanessa's life—her personal life, her professional life, her spiritual life, and her family life—over the last three to five years. Each area is substandard according to her. Vanessa fears she'll be unable to escape this downward spiral.

At this point, I told her, "Let's not only look at each one of these four areas. Let's figure out how you got there. Let's talk about what you did to get here, what you did to get here, what you did to get here, and what you did to get here," and I mentioned four different areas in her life. Each time, it was the same behavior and the same decision-making process that landed Vanessa in the same negative position in each aspect of her life. Therefore, when we pinpointed the primary area that needed modification more than anything else in her life, it was the same thread that ran through her all of her dissatisfaction and unhappiness.

Vanessa was negligent. In each instance, there came a point where she took her eye off the ball and somebody else had to fix a problem, or that problem didn't get fixed. There was never a time where she said, "This is my responsibility. I have to make it work." For example, she worked in retail store, and her district manager and her regional manager were both making things more difficult for her than they should have been. Although Vanessa's sales were good, and she was doing well at the store, these managers weren't supporting her advancement or any of the things she needed. She was unable to persevere or push through the office politics (which so many of us have to deal with), and instead allowed herself to become their punching bag.

Vanessa's reaction was to be hands off. She told me, "I just don't say anything anymore. I don't document anything anymore. I don't challenge anything anymore. I'm no longer trying to find a way to provide the higher-ups with information about the dysfunction that I see. I don't mobilize colleagues to collectively address the issues that affect us all. I just sit back and hope that things will change."

So our first step was to identify one area—in this case, her work—where Vanessa could begin, without being insubordinate or combative, to figure out strategic ways to try to control the ship herself. As it happened, the chief operating officer of the company was planning to tour all the various stores, so when he sent an e-mail to all employees at her store saying how much he was looking forward to coming there, Vanessa decided to e-mail him back. She wrote, "I know you're coming to observe our store. I look forward to hearing what you're going to say about the direction of the company. I would love to be able to have just ten minutes of your time to share with you some great ideas that I have for ways I believe we can be more effective."

It was an incredibly positive note. Vanessa didn't talk about any of the negative things that were bothering her. Instead, she found a way to assert her value to the store to someone who was even higher up than her district manager or regional manager—and without going over their heads to complain about anything. Instead, she took advantage of this opportunity of the COO's visit to ask for an opportunity to talk to him. Even better, he said he really liked her ideas and that he'd like to see her begin to implement them. That was a very small success for Vanessa, but it was a step in the right direction, on her journey to her personal best.

Finally, the reason she was able to send that e-mail to the COO was that she'd written herself a memo that her BlackBerry would send to her every day at noon and 3. It said: "Assert yourself." Vanessa had mapped her journey and used her transformational calendar. She was on her way to achieving more at work and being happier in general.

Develop your strategy for reaching your destination. You'll find yourself stepping into each transition of your journey with confidence instead of second-guessing every ill-planned step. As public speaker and author Larry Elder says: "A goal without a plan is just a wish." Move forward doing more than simply wishing for your best to come. Create the strategic plan that will truly get you there.

CHAPTER 9

Transform Mistakes into Opportunity

Okay, you've come a long way on this journey. You've identified what you are not, created a picture of yourself as a whole person, determined where you want this person to go, made a leap of faith, created your strategy, and started walking. Then you mess it all up. What do you do now? One more thing before we even start: you need to find a mirror. Seriously, stop here and find a mirror. It doesn't matter the size or shape, but I want you to look at yourself and tell yourself:

I AM GOING TO MAKE MISTAKES.

Remember it. It's critical not only to your advancement to your personal best, but to your very survival. Knowing that you're going to make mistakes sets you up to overcome and move beyond them before you make them because if you accept the fact that you're going to make mistakes, you'll be emotionally prepared to deal with the psychological pain associated with temporary failure and setbacks.

Are mistakes fun? Nope. Are they the best way to get something done? Not usually. Are they ideal, something to be coveted and sought after? No way, shape, or form, but they're not the end of the world, either. The best way to wrap your head around learning from mistakes is to realize two very important things. First, not every mistake is the same. Just like there is bad cholesterol and good cholesterol, bad debt and good debt, bad stress and good stress, there are bad mistakes and good mistakes. The trick is in knowing the difference. This chapter will help you do that.

Second, not every mistake is bad. Have you ever heard the phrase "happy accident?" That's kind of what happened to Steven Spielberg, director of *Jaws,* and Dr. Pemberton, a pharmacist who invented a headache remedy and ended up inventing Coca-Cola. What started out as a high-tech shark movie turned into something completely different—and better. What started out as a hangover remedy turned into something completely different—and better. Your job as we move through this chapter will be not just to know which mistake is which, but to believe that every mistake has something to teach us.

Our mistakes are sometimes very hard to categorize. There are work mistakes, relationship mistakes, health mistakes, diet mistakes, social mistakes, and grammar mistakes. It seems that there are as many kinds of mistakes as there are ways to make mistakes. You can stop counting, because when it comes to mistakes, there are only two kinds: avoidable and unavoidable.

Intentional Mistakes, Ignorant Mistakes, and Inescapable Mistakes

Most of our mistakes fall into one of three classes, which I call the three "I"s: intentional mistakes, ignorant mistakes, and inescapable mistakes. The three "I"s are mistakes we are inevitably forced to deal with on our journey. Let's begin with a brief description of each type of mistake, and I'll offer strategies required to move past them.

Intentional mistakes are those things you do that you know are a bad idea from the beginning—but you do them anyway. You give yourself three or four reasons why you shouldn't make the decision, and you may even have played out some of the consequences in your mind. However, you overruled your good instincts. You wanted to date that person, or you wanted to take that trip, and you had to buy that car. When the sky starts to fall and you are up to your neck in storm clouds, there is no one to blame, no one to look at but the person looking back at you in the mirror. You did this with full knowledge, and now you must use that same knowledge to make better decisions next time.

Ignorant mistakes are those errors that result from a decision you made without having all the information you needed. Perhaps you rushed to make the decision, failed to gather all the necessary information, depended too much on someone's advice—or any of a thousand other reasons that indicate you acted before you fully assessed the situation or understood the next step. Most of the mistakes people make fall into this category. In this chapter, we'll walk through some exercises in patience, discernment, and analysis that will help you make empowered, and not just impassioned, decisions.

Inescapable mistakes are those mistakes that you really couldn't have done anything to avoid. You gathered all the information you could, and made responsible decisions that considered your vision. Still, you made the wrong decision.

No matter the type of mistake, we're all going to make them. The reality is that no matter how visionary, smart, or driven we are, there's an innate imperfection that we're cloaked with because we are human. I believe that this imperfection is a built-in ego check system installed by God (the creator, the universe, or whatever you believe created you). Can you imagine how inflated our egos would be if we were perfect? Some of us are difficult enough to deal with, and we're flawed; imagine how difficult we'd be to deal with if we were perfect! This built-in ego check, on its best day, helps us realize that we cannot do it all alone, that we're not the beginning and end of creation, and that there's an inherent value in other people. These unavoidable mistakes make us human. So take a deep breath, embrace that sigh of relief, and say aloud: I don't have to be perfect.

Moving Beyond Your Mistakes

Understand this: even as we make avoidable mistakes repeatedly—and even our share of unavoidable mistakes—we *can* embrace them as lessons. I don't buy into the notion, "Well, if such and such happened, it was meant to be." Don't tell me it was meant to be that you got busted for traffic violations, got your girlfriend pregnant, got caught smoking a joint in the club parking lot, dropped out of school, or got fired from your job for poor performance. 'Fess up and say, "I messed up! I knew better and I did it anyway. It's all my fault." Being able to learn from a situation doesn't mean it was predestined.

Okay, fine, great. You've admitted it, now move on. The reality is that it doesn't have to keep you down forever. This mistake, that mistake—all mistakes—can be used as powerful lessons. It doesn't mean you have to make the same mistake three times to learn. Make the mistake once, learn from it, avoid it next time, and move on. Don't be ashamed. Don't beat yourself up. Don't call yourself a "loser." And, whatever you do, don't hide the mistake.

If assessing the types of mistakes you make were the only step in this process, most of you would be masters of manifesting your best. The truth is that identifying the type of mistake is the easy part. How you move beyond that mistake is the hard part and essential to achieving your personal best. Yet I hear so many people say (and I myself have said), "I admitted it, didn't I?" The words seem to make sense: accepting responsibility for what you did wrong should allow you to begin the process of moving beyond the mistake, right? However, accepting the mistake and owning it are not the same as owning the behavior that caused that mistake and correcting it.

I don't know about you, but this was a difficult one for me. I was good for apologizing for the act and continuing the behavior almost intentionally. Many of us are not sorry for the mistake, but sorry we were caught or called to the table. Too often, we fail to own both the mistake and the behavior that caused it.

Therefore, to move to the next level, it's essential that you embrace the error and rebuke the behavior. You must walk out of the acknowledged mistake, prepared to answer three questions:

1. "What did I do wrong in this situation?"

2. "Why did I do it that way and what was I trying to gain?"

3. "How can I think, behave, and respond differently the next time this situation comes my way?"

These questions are all aimed at understanding and correcting the problem. Although they're not difficult, they challenge us to realize why we act in certain ways and set us up to transform ourselves. (I'll discuss them in more detail later.)

There's one key factor to consider when moving from mistake to manifestation, and that is forgiveness. I mean self-forgiveness. For many, this is the most difficult part. Forgiveness is a challenge because we often don't realize that we're holding ourselves in a prison of un-forgiveness in the first place.

Failing to forgive yourself for a mistake you've made takes on different forms. You may go out of your way to please someone you once wronged, as if you were indebted to that person forever. You may find yourself unable to celebrate small or large personal victories because you focus on some imperfection and the mistake that illuminates it. Perhaps you're someone who repeatedly claims that you've done something wrong because you fear hearing someone else say it first. This, too, is an indication that you have not forgiven yourself for one or perhaps a multitude of mistakes you've made. Finally, you may be unable to move beyond because you're afraid you'll make another mistake or even repeat the same mistake. You don't move at all because you think, "If I don't move, I can't make a mistake." The most painful aspect of being in one of these places is that even when the person you wronged has forgiven you, you still hold onto the shame and fail to forgive yourself.

Today, you have to free yourself. Let's begin by looking at some of the mistakes people make every day and how each of these situations could have been handled better, and how you can deal with any mistakes you might have made or may make in the future. The goal is for you to walk out of this chapter having admitted, assessed, attained, adjusted, and absolved yourself. Then you'll be free to manifest.

Admitting to Intentional Mistakes

Your goal should be to not fret so much about making the same mistakes repeatedly—we're only human—but to learn from each mistake so you can avoid doing so much damage control *after* the avoidable mistake is made.

If you're horrible on first dates and always say the wrong thing, step back and, next time, let him do all the talking. If you're too aggressive at work and always overstep, learn how to delegate and let others be part of your team. If you keep partying too hard the night before an exam and always test horribly the next day, learn from your avoidable mistake and stop partying too hard the night before an exam.

Or how about this? Party *after* the exam.

As mentioned earlier, intentional mistakes are mistakes you make when you know you shouldn't do something, but you do it anyway. This can be something as benign as buying something you really can't afford (and then having to deal with the debt for a long time to come), or it can be as serious as committing a crime.

An extreme example of this behavior that I've seen personally is from a man named Steve, whom my dad met in a support group. My dad has inoperable macular degeneration, and is legally blind. He can still see to some extent, and recently completed a program that has enabled him to drive again if he wears a special type of glasses. When his loss of sight really started to affect his day-to-day living nearly nine years ago, my dad joined a few support groups, which is where he met Steve.

Steve became blind when he shot himself in an attempt to commit suicide. He has serious bouts of depression because it's obviously not easy to be blind (especially when not born that way), and his depression is made worse because Steve knows this was something that he and he alone caused. He can deal with the fact that he went through a rough emotional time and that his life was difficult, but he has no one else to blame for his blindness—there's no one he can point to, there's no one else at fault. Moreover, he didn't accidentally shoot himself, so he is forced to deal not only with the reality of never seeing again, but also with the painful reality that he caused his blindness, by his own hand, with his own gun. That is a huge mistake with huge ramifications to deal with.

Steve has joined several support groups that have helped him learn to live as a visually impaired person. He has a seeing-eye dog. He lives on his own, has a girlfriend, has a job, and functions like you and I function on a daily basis. He is managing the physical and logistical challenges of being blind. However, on most days, Steve's biggest challenge is dealing with the psychological aspect of his situation.

Steve recently confided in my dad how depressed he was and how he just didn't know how to deal with his depression. My dad told him, "I'm living with terminal cancer and am blind, so you're not going to get a pity party from me. This is your life, and thank God, you have one. Clearly, you're here to accomplish something because, although you tried to take your life, it didn't work. You've been given an opportunity to continue to live, and to experience and enjoy life, although not in the same way you would have before. You also have an opportunity to give to others, because you have more to share than you realize."

On an extreme level, Steve is in a place that many of us are: we don't know how to deal with the harsh reality of a mistake we made, and we can't blame it on anybody or anything else. Fortunately, not too many of you reading this book have had to deal with a failed suicide attempt, but I want to use Steve's story to illustrate, in the strongest possible way, that some of the intentional mistakes we make can literally blind us to what our future is supposed to be. Many of us are no longer able to see where it is we're supposed to go—where our personal best actually is—because the shame, the hurt, and the pain of whatever mistake we've made has put our entire world on pause.

Although most people's mistakes are not as life-changing as Steve's, whatever your particular mistake was or is, it probably seems insurmountable. For example, I have a friend named Cheryl who got pregnant in college. She hadn't planned to get pregnant; she was only twenty years old, in her junior year, and a premed: her passion was medical research, because she wanted to help people by finding cures for life-threatening illnesses rather than just treating patients. Cheryl's family was also highly educated, and the women in particular were very accomplished: her mother was a doctor, one aunt was an engineer, and her sister was a professional ballerina. Like them, Cheryl had big plans for her life, and having a child at age twenty had not been part of those plans.

Because the women in her family were so accomplished, and had walked such a straight and narrow path, their mere examples made Cheryl feel as if her life were over. When she told them she was pregnant, they told her they couldn't believe that she did that to herself. Cheryl really didn't need her family to tell her this. She was already feeling bad enough because her pregnancy was derailing her college education. She realized that the mistake she'd made by getting pregnant was going to change her life dramatically.

Because she was a responsible person (on most occasions), she began to do everything she could to make sure she'd be able to provide for her child. She left college, intending to take a year off to have the baby and take care of her child during the baby's first year, and then return to school. Also, Cheryl was fortunate because the baby's father was involved and helped her during the pregnancy and after the baby was born. But he also wasn't really ready to start a family: he was only nineteen years old, and also in college. He didn't drop out of college, as Cheryl did, but stopped going full-time so he could work part-time and attend classes part-time. Additionally although Cheryl's family disapproved, they did not abandon her, so she had financial help to take care of her baby and return to school if she wanted. In other words, she didn't have to handle the ramifications of her mistake all by herself.

Nevertheless, Cheryl was consumed by her mistake. She had some resentment toward the baby's father, and she was angry with herself for not having been more careful before she was ready to have a child. They intentionally had unprotected sex, neglected to get birth control, and spit in the face of all her mother had taught her by way of Christian teaching on sex. She was unable to see beyond those mistakes. In fact, once the baby was born, all she talked about was being there for the baby. And why not? That is what she was supposed to do. However, she felt she had to cancel, not modify or postpone, everything else...college, pre-med, the rest of what she'd planned to do. Needless to say, she didn't go back to college a year later.

Although Cheryl did not deny that she bore part of the blame for her situation, she was incapable of forgiving herself. For about two years, she was unable to see beyond her mistake. She talked incessantly about where she should've been at that time if she'd not made this mistake: "If I hadn't messed up, I would've been graduating college now. I should be applying for med schools right now. I can't believe that I'm not where I expected to be in my life." She just couldn't get past the fact that she was on a different path than the one she'd been working toward her whole young life.

At the same time, she had a beautiful daughter whom she named Layla. Cheryl was a good mother. She loved her little girl, and treated Layla very well. Whatever resentment she felt was not directed at her baby. However, she was still not able to say to herself, "Wait a minute. This is not how I intended my life to be. This was not my plan, but I can move on from here."

When Layla was two years old, Cheryl wanted to get her into a prestigious private preschool—which had one of those endless waiting lists. Cheryl ran into a friend, Erica, whom she had known from college, and who was working as an admissions counselor at that school. Erica naturally asked Cheryl what she was doing now and where she was going to school, and when Cheryl told her that she hadn't gone back, Erica asked her why not. Cheryl explained that she felt her responsibility was to Layla, not to the dreams she'd previously had about finishing college and going to medical school and becoming a researcher or anything beyond a mom. Cheryl felt all that had changed, and now she had to make sure that Layla fulfilled her dreams.

Erica couldn't believe what Cheryl was telling her, and she challenged Cheryl on that. She said, "You're only twenty-two years old. Your life isn't over! You were a dean's list student before you became pregnant. You were involved in organizations. You had a great social life. You say you're no longer that person just because you had a baby earlier than you wanted to. But that's not the person I knew." Erica also told Cheryl that one of the things that helped her (Erica) get through school was the example Cheryl had set when they were both freshman. "Watching you was what helped me learn the study habits, the discipline, and the focus needed to get me through college successfully." Erica also encouraged Cheryl to realize that investing in and making a priority of Layla's future did not have to happen to the detriment of her own.

Interestingly, Erica did not say to Cheryl, "You should've been working on your doctorate by now," or "You could've been a researcher at the National Institutes of Health by now." Erica wasn't trying to pressure Cheryl onto some unrealistic track to professional perfection; instead, she just wanted to point out to Cheryl that one mistake should not be the end of the world. She told Cheryl, "You can do more than you're doing. You're not just a mom. There are so many other things in your life to which you should be pushing. You've used this pregnancy and your baby as an excuse for why you're not doing these."

Hearing Erica tell her all these things was like a slap in the face, and it brought Cheryl back to reality. She finally said to herself, "What am I doing here? Why have I put myself in this prison over this mistake? I've accepted my responsibility and I'm caring for my child, but I also need to take care of me and what I want for my life." Erica was able to help Cheryl see beyond her mistake and to recognize that she still had the rest of her life to live. Cheryl told me she realized, "If I can't wipe the sleep out of my eyes and see beyond the mistake I made, I'm always going to be sitting in the dark and will never move forward." That's what we all need to realize: we can't let one mistake, no matter what it is, be the end of our road. Instead, we need to keep traveling on our journey to achieve our personal best.

Accepting Ignorant Mistakes

Ignorant mistakes are a little bit easier to deal with than intentional mistakes because they're not the result of intentionally poor judgment, or a selfish desire to have something, or because you've done something you know you shouldn't have done. For this reason, these are easier mistakes to forgive yourself for, not beat yourself up about, and to use as an opportunity to learn and grow.

For example, when I started my first business, I had absolutely no idea what I was doing. All I knew was that I wanted to work for myself. I knew that I had to file some paperwork and to get a lawyer, but I was completely ignorant about the accounting side of a business. I was making revenue, I was keeping my books, and I was doing everything I thought I was supposed to be doing. Admittedly, I didn't have an accountant at the time because I was trying to save money and do as much as I could by myself. I thought using QuickBooks to keep track of my expenses and revenue was enough. But, as a 1099 employee on every single contract I had, I was unaware of how much money I had to set aside to pay my taxes. And although I thought I was withholding enough, I wasn't—and at the end of my first year in business, I was hit with a big bill from the IRS. Unbelievably, my tax bill for the business and my personal taxes was in the six figures...which, of course, I didn't have.

After beating myself up, unable to believe I could do that, and after recognizing that it was going to take me forever to get out of that hole, I contacted a lawyer who specialized in tax law. He helped me make a deal with the IRS to spread out what I owed. It took me three years to pay it back, but I realized that I was not going to stop doing business because I had made that mistake. I said to myself, "I'm not going to close my doors. Instead, I'm going to shift gears. I'll dissolve this company, pay the taxes, then start another company and run it the right way."

Now I have an incredible accountant in addition to my lawyer. What I did is an extreme example of a mistake made out of ignorance. (Don't let it happen to you: if you work for yourself, you need to set aside so much more money than you think you'll need for the tax man, because no matter how much you set aside, it's almost never enough!) I ended up spending ten times what an accountant would have cost trying to save a little money by not having an accountant, but I learned from that mistake, I forgave myself and moved on, dedicated and committed to never make that mistake again.

Dealing with Inescapable Mistakes

Finally, in addition to intentional and ignorant mistakes, there are also inescapable mistakes—when you think you've done everything you possibly could do and should do, and something still goes wrong. We've all been there, so I know you know what I mean.

For example, I have a friend named Michelle, whom I've known for years. We met when I was president of student government at my college and she was president of student government at another university. We had an interesting relationship, because she is white and grew up in a very racist home, but Michelle didn't agree with her parents' racism, and she challenged it from a very young age. We became very good friends and at times we sought each other's counsel.

During college, Michelle met a man at church. Don seemed to be the ideal guy: a college graduate, a young lawyer who worked long hours to make his way up in the firm, and a member of several nonprofit organizations to which he volunteered his time. Michelle and Don started dating. After a year and a half, they got engaged, and two years later they got married. They seemed like the perfect couple: they went out regularly, had a healthy social life, and attended church together. About a year into their marriage, she went on a business trip for her sales job, and since she'd been on the road frequently during that quarter, she decided to come home early and surprise Don. When she walked into the house, she heard noises upstairs, where she found Don in bed with another man.

Clearly, this was not what she expected, and it wasn't what she'd expected from her marriage. When she told me about it, she kept repeating, "I can't believe I didn't know Don was gay. I did everything right: we knew each other for a long time before we got married; we were friends before we even dated. I went to church with him, I met his family, I met all his friends. There just didn't seem to have been any telltale signs. To come in and find this happening in my house, I don't understand how I could have made such a mistake."

Michelle called me about what had happened because I knew Don, too. He'd also been a student leader when we were in college. Michelle asked me if I thought she was crazy, and she wanted to know if there were any warning signs that she could have seen that would have given her any hint that Don was interested in men. I reassured her by telling her, "There is *nothing* you could have done differently. You asked all the right questions. You did what you could. You just didn't know, and he didn't tell you. He may have been trying to deal with his feelings toward men, or he may have known he was gay and failed to share that with you."

It took her about a year to gain clarity on what had happened to her marriage. She and Don went through counseling. He ultimately admitted that he had known he had sexual desires for men for about a year. He knew before they got married, but he didn't want to admit it to himself. He thought he could deal with it, and hoped that the church and prayer would help him.

Her biggest issue with him was that he didn't tell her, that he allowed her to make a decision that would affect the rest of her life without giving her the information she needed to make the right decision for herself. That's what made her choose divorce. She told him, "If you had discovered this after we got married, and didn't know how to tell me, that would be one thing. But you knew before we got married and kept it from me, and I can't forgive you for that."

Michelle understood that she made the decision to marry based on everything she thought she knew about Don, and therefore she refused to beat herself up for marrying him. She wasn't going to second-guess herself. The issue for her was Don's dishonesty; she didn't take it as a rejection or assume that something was wrong with her. She recognized that she made an inescapable mistake, not because she was inherently flawed as a person or had flawed judgment. She'd gotten to know Don as a friend before dating him, they'd dated for years, were engaged for more than a year, she'd met all his friends and family, and there was nothing unusual that would have indicated his interest in men. There was no way she could have known that this marriage was a mistake, so she wasn't going to beat herself up about it any longer. The real issue? Don hadn't been honest with her. She recognized this was a not a preventable mistake, nor was it the result of inherently flawed judgment.

Although Michelle did not begin dating again for quite some time, her outlook was healthy. She told me, "I know that I want to date and be in a relationship again. I need to get over Don, but I'm not going to put myself in prison." She eventually did remarry, and about five months ago, she and her new husband had their first baby. Michelle and her new husband have an incredible relationship based on an enormous amount of transparency. It wouldn't have been possible for her to be in a relationship with someone who was secretive or apprehensive about being aboveboard about absolutely everything in his life. She and her new husband are very much alike: they both want someone who isn't afraid to talk about everything, and they're very happy.

Michelle even talks to Don every once in a while. They're almost friends again because Don was, after all, the man she'd planned to spend the rest of her life with. She doesn't hate him, she's forgiven him for what happened, and is in a very healthy and happy place because she recognized that she'd made a mistake through no fault of her own.

With that understanding, Michelle was able to ask herself, "How can I move forward and not make the same type of mistake again? What can I do differently? What kinds of questions can I ask? What kind of counseling do I need? What kind of relationship environment can I create?" One of the things she learned, by asking herself these questions, was that she probably had not created an environment in which Don would have felt comfortable discussing his realization that he might be gay. Although Michelle wasn't homophobic or antigay, she had made some careless comments that probably prevented Don from saying anything about the new feelings he was having when they were still dating. So even though Don was responsible for not being honest with Michelle, Michelle also realized that she needed to accept responsibility for not being open to more honest conversation.

How to Move Beyond Your Mistakes to Achieve Your Personal Best

What I'm trying to point out in this chapter is that it's not enough to admit you made a mistake, as Cheryl did. Instead, you must do what Michelle did and move beyond beating yourself up about it, not just admit your mistake but to actually take responsibility for it. To do that, you need to ask and answer three critical questions.

What did I do wrong?

Asking this question is not an indication that you're blaming yourself. It essentially means that you're trying to identify behavior that you can improve on to create the kind of environment in which you won't make this kind of mistake again. That's what Michelle did when she realized she'd made antigay jokes—she'd created an environment where Don would have felt uncomfortable discussing his realization with her. It didn't force her to take on blame that wasn't hers, but it illustrated a way she could become more aware.

Why did I do it that way? What was I trying to gain?

I think these questions are even more important than the first, because they go beyond simple action to intention. For example, if Michelle were to ask herself, "Why did I create a situation where Don felt he couldn't tell me how he was feeling? What did I gain from that?" She'd realize that she hadn't really done anything wrong because her mistake wasn't an intentional, deliberate act . Since she didn't know Don might be gay, she didn't realize that her off-color jokes might prevent him from being completely honest with her. Yes, she'd made inappropriate comments, and she learned from that mistake—she's learned to be even more open-minded than she thought she was.

Similarly, if Cheryl were to ask herself, "Why did I allow myself to get pregnant? What was I trying to gain? Why did I embark on a sexual relationship and not take better care to prevent getting pregnant?" She might answer that she was looking for affection that she could have gotten in another way, or that she became sexually involved with the father (who had his own set of questions to ask and process to go through) because she was emotionally lazy or lonely. After all, college is hard, and often when people are in a new environment, they get involved with someone as a crutch, to have someone to lean on.

Forgiveness is what allows you to move forward. Some people say, "I forgive, but I don't forget." I'm not certain that's possible. Forgetting does not mean that you put it out of your mind and it's forever lost in an abyss of the past and never comes to mind again. Instead, I believe forgetting means that you're not constantly thinking about your mistake anymore. I know people who've done something to themselves or somebody has done something to them, and not a week goes by that they don't intentionally recall that, because they want to maintain some sense of emotion around that event. Those people really do not forget it. Recalling it every now and again is not the same thing as intentionally holding on to something and regularly bringing it to mind. Allowing yourself to forgive yourself and forget what you did is essential to freeing yourself to move forward. When you don't forgive yourself, you can't move on.

How can I think, behave, and respond differently next time?

Part of the process of moving beyond a mistake to manifest your best is to process why you did it and to determine what you can do differently so you won't make that mistake again. When you start challenging yourself to think and act differently, that's the doorway to forgiveness because then you're saying to yourself, "I'm not going to do this again. I'm not going to go in this direction again. I know this because I've created something to help push me in the opposite direction." In addition, when you're able to focus on the question, "What am I going to do differently?" you're giving yourself room to become better, and to move forward on your journey toward your personal best. In contrast, when you focus on "What did I do?" you're not giving yourself any room to change.

That's what this is all about: creating a new way of doing something so that you can forgive yourself. Forgiving yourself gives you the freedom to do things in a new way.

Often people say, "I forgive you" or "I forgive myself," but I believe forgiveness is the acknowledgment that you're sorry enough to behave differently so that it doesn't happen again. I won't forgive you if I think you're going to do it again. I don't forgive you because you say you're sorry. I forgive myself because I believe that I have sincerely acknowledged that what I did was wrong. Because what I did was wrong, I have to atone for it. Part of atoning for it is not only accepting that it was wrong, but creating a new methodology so that it doesn't happen again. Because of that process, I can forgive myself, because I know I'm not going down the same road.

Cheryl told me what Erica had said about the effect Cheryl had had on Erica's life. I said, "The question you have to ask yourself is, 'Do you want to forgive yourself for wasting your life, or do you want to forgive yourself for being in a situation that caused you to take a detour?' At the end of the day, I think it's a lot healthier to forgive yourself for a detour than for wasting a whole bunch of years blaming yourself for something that isn't really blocking you from becoming your best."

Once Cheryl processed that, she decided to move on, and told herself, "Things aren't that bad. I have a beautiful baby girl, whom I love. Layla's father is helping to take care of her. We're raising her together. My family is supportive and hasn't thrown me out to deal with my situation on my own. More important, I have a vision of what I want to be, and who I want to be, and I want to become that." With that realization, Cheryl went back to college, and she'll be graduating soon.

Today, she doesn't talk about becoming pregnant as a detour; she talks about what it is she needs to do in the future. She realizes that her unplanned pregnancy was just a detour, one that made her take longer to get through school than she would have if she hadn't had her baby. Cheryl had the ability to manifest the next phase of her journey because she forgave herself.

Some of you may be thinking how lucky Cheryl was, because maybe you don't have a supportive family, or the financial means, or someone to help take care of your child, or whatever situation you're facing. But most people have some resources. You need to forgive yourself and start looking at what you do have, even if it isn't as much as Cheryl had. You have something, even if you don't have what you think you should. I think there are times when people look at the mistakes they've made and think that what they have is not enough—when, in most cases, what they have is exactly enough for them to get to the next place. You just have to acknowledge that what you have is enough for you to move forward on your journey toward your own personal best.

Now, here's the thing about unavoidable mistakes: we have to deal with them if we're ever going to manifest our purposes. Meanwhile, our avoidable mistakes are going to have to be kept to a minimum. It's a one-two punch, a dual decision. Do your best to avoid the mistakes you can and be your best in the face of those mistakes you can't avoid.

No matter the resources, the support base, or the mistake, there's no excuse for stopping your journey. Even falling on your face is moving forward, so get up, brush yourself off, forgive yourself, and use that mistake as a springboard to manifest the next phase of your journey to the best place in your life.

CHAPTER 10

Conquer Conflict Crossroads

As you continue to make your way on this journey, you'll inevitably reach what I call the Conflict Crossroad. This is where your current mediocre, substandard, old life slams into the *potentially new you* and you must make difficult and often life-altering decisions if you're to move forward and fulfill your vision. These are decisions that test your resolve, that look you dead in the eye and ask if you're for real or just playing. These crossroads challenge whether you should have ever started this journey in the first place and force you to answer the question, "Do I *really* want to be my best?" Unfortunately, many of us punk out at these Conflict Crossroads and exit off the highway to our best, in exchange for a rest stop of comfort and convenience that goes nowhere.

Have you ever had a flinching contest? My friends and I used to have these all the time when we were kids. Basically, you and your friend stood facing each other and did increasingly, just short of violent things to each other. Almost kicked, almost punched, almost threw a soda can until the other person flinched. Whoever flinched first, naturally, lost.

While this is juvenile, looking back, this is how I picture people when they face a Conflict Crossroad. They flinch in the face of challenge before ever moving forward. They don't move through the intersection between what was and what could be, and in the process, they give up too soon, and never follow through to change their lives.

Flinching, of course, is just the physical equivalent of mentally or emotionally punking out when real opportunity for personal evolution stares you in the face. What if Will Smith blinked and thought all he could ever do was sing family-friendly hip-hop? What if Barack Obama flinched and thought the world wasn't ready to have an African American president? What if Kanye West decided that being a producer was good enough? What if some of our families gave up on us after we messed up for the fifth time?

The Big Flinch, of course, is a lot more than just not blinking when a friend threatens to slap your face. What if your Conflict Crossroad is at the bank, signing on the dotted line of that big loan you need to start your new company? What if it's at the altar, starting a new life with your perfect partner? What if it's at the pitch meeting, as you introduce your movie treatment to Hollywood bigwigs? Or what if it's choosing between an opportunity *you* want and one that your family thinks is best?

Flinching at a Conflict Crossroad is like quitting just before the start of a championship race. How will you know what it feels like to win if you never enter the race, cross the line, and see what it's like on the other side of victory?

My goal is to teach you not to flinch.

In fact, I want you to do the exact opposite: face those Conflict Crossroads with your eyes wide open, curious and courageous about this next leg of the journey to your personal best.

Conflict Crossroads are the inevitable pathways. You can't avoid these crossroads, no matter how hard—or how often—you flinch. But it's time to man or woman up: this chapter will help you take advantage of these showdowns and learn to welcome the changes.

Confronting the Conflict Between Now and Then

On the road to manifesting your best, one of the most challenging aspects of progress is confronting conflict. Conflict is never pretty. In fact, many of us spend our whole lives working extra hard to simply avoid conflict.

Think about it: how often have you written an e-mail instead of picking up the phone, all so you wouldn't have to confront your boss, your spouse, your soon-to-be ex-lover. There are always decisions you have to make that take you from one point in life to the next. Remember when it was time to declare your college major? That was a Conflict Crossroad. What about when you decided to propose? Or when you decided to join the organization that none of your friends were a part of? Or took your first job? All of these represent Conflict Crossroads.

The problem people have with Conflict Crossroads is that the more of them you pass through, the more you know how hard they're going to be, because conflict typically means change. Life changes the minute you start working, and not always for the better. We are torn between the lost innocence of our youth and truly being financially responsible for ourselves.

Most of us in fact, want to avoid change, not embrace it.

We avoid the chances we have to rise to life's challenges because we're scared of the mistakes we *might* make. Not only are all mistakes opportunities, but we can learn from them if we move forward through the conflict.

Making Hard Decisions

What happens when you decide to transform your life? What happens when you're forced to change or grow in a way that is so disruptive or destructive that you can't deny its affect on your present reality?

There are times in our lives when there are subtle shifts and evolutions that we don't even notice them: the way our faces age gradually over time, the way our savings accounts slowly accrue interest, the way our mortgages eventually get paid off. Well, you don't miss that one happening, but you get it. Don't be fooled, however. Conflict Crossroads are the exact *opposite* of that. There's no way to avoid them or not acknowledge them. They force you to change, one way or the other.

You may ask why, because change (especially self-change) is one of the most difficult things we face. It consumes us—both its promise for something new and our fear of something new. Whether it's the "something new" part or the change itself, we just can't seem to muscle past the gag reflex that comes whenever change rears its threatening—if not opportunistic—head. All the steps you've taken thus far have fundamentally changed who you are. And that's why people get scared, why they lose heart. Why we absolutely hate change

A Change Is Gonna Come—Whether We Like It or Not

So often change is *forced upon us* versus being *instigated by us*. The world moves so quickly and situations occur so rapidly that we're forced to internalize change at a rapid pace. Let's face it, the world is crazy and change is inherent in it. Because of this we often don't acknowledge the change that happens as much as we just flow with the tide, ending up in whatever destination we're dropped into. Think of how we most often change: it's generally due not so much to ourselves but is more because of the will of someone or something else.

We move from our hometown to a bigger city because there are more opportunities there. We pick up new habits not necessarily because we enjoy them, but because our spouse, mate, or lover has them. Even what we read, see, and wear is dictated by others more in the know—or so they tell us—than ourselves.

However, at Conflict Crossroads, we're forced as individuals to do things that usually have graver consequences than what we view as the everyday challenges of normal life.

We must change to become our personal best. No magazine article or horoscope can tell you how to do this, and you won't get there by riding a wave of hope or simple faith. Even the Bible says that faith *without* works is dead. This is no easy feat.

No one has been able to walk into or manifest their best without having to make decisions that pushed them, challenged them, changed their very environment, shifted their belief system, and, in many cases, invited in or forced out close family members and friends. Difficult decisions like these determine whether we're worthy and, in many cases, prepared to walk consistently in a new personal direction.

Take a man like Martin Luther King, Jr.; conflict was something he welcomed. He embraced it as his cross to bear, understanding that his personal best was connected to the destiny of a huge population in the United States and abroad. Was it fun for him to go through so many Conflict Crossroads? Fun, I doubt, but purposeful, absolutely. Here was a man filled with the desire to manifest to the fullest all of the God-given ability he was blessed with, through passion and commitment.

With so many people depending on his leadership and guidance—with our very country changing by the second—I'm sure he passed through as many Conflict Crossroads as there were days on the calendar.

Look at any great leader—Winston Churchill, Patrice Lumumba, Mahatma Gandhi, Nelson Mandela, Mother Teresa—and ask yourself how many Conflict Crossroads were enough? Think of our elected leaders, the titans of industry, or the enlightened gurus to whom the rest of us flock for leadership and guidance. For that matter, let's look at those other folks like you and me. Is the kid around the corner who's served a buffet of gangs, drugs, and other distractions faced with any fewer Conflict Crossroads? Are a dozen Conflict Crossroads enough? On the other hand, is that just what leaders and "citizens" alike endure before breakfast on an average day?

The thing about change is that it's inevitable—it's going to come, whether we like it or not. We can either get out in front of it and make the change, or we can stay behind it—hoping naively to avoid it—and let the change happen *to* us instead of *for* us.

Look at how we age. Aging is simply inevitable. In other words, like change, it's going to happen, whether we want it to or not. Now, there are two ways to face aging: either negligently, by doing nothing to take care of your mind and body, or actively, by aggressively taking care of yourself.

Those who neglect themselves, in fact, are doomed to age more quickly than those who actively live a healthier lifestyle. They don't exercise, so they lose muscle tone, skin vitality, and bone density. They don't eat right, so they raise their cholesterol, heart rate, and blood pressure. All of these signs of aging also contribute to aging more quickly.

On the other hand, those who age on their own terms—who actively court change—exercise to make their muscles and bones strong, eat right to keep their cholesterol and blood pressure low, and take preventive measures, like wearing sunscreen and using replenishing agents to avoid wrinkles. Therefore, not only do they not appear older, they actually feel younger.

Now, the difference is merely biological, not chronological. A fifty-five-year-old man who ignores his health is just as old as a fifty-five-year-old man who actively takes care of himself, yet the two are not the same. One is a victim of aging and one is a victor over aging. One feared change, the other faced it—and welcomed it.

Which one are you?

Follow the Signs to Your Conflict Crossroads

Conflict Crossroads manifest themselves in any number of ways. Sometimes they even challenge who's in our lives. Are we prepared to marry the person who's supposed to be our mate? Are we prepared to remove certain people from our lives, the people who are in our way, and possibly create a barrier to our next stage of life? You'll find out at the Conflict Crossroads.

These crossroads often create an intersection between complacency and possibility, geographically speaking. Are you up to moving from one area of your life for opportunity, be it a graduate program that doesn't exist where you live, or a job, person, or opportunity that doesn't exist where you live? Don't worry if you don't know just yet; you'll find out at the Conflict Crossroads.

No matter what and how Conflict Crossroads manifest themselves, they are the ultimate pass/fail test. There are no incompletes. Either you successfully move beyond the current conflict or you stay stuck where you are. You can't move forward if you don't deal with it. Ignoring it places you in a perpetual purgatory. While you may not move back, you definitely aren't moving forward. Therefore, you can either do something and change for the better, or do nothing and stay where you are. Which, along the road to your best, loosely translates into moving farther away from the destination you claim you want to reach.

Remember, regardless of where your best is, or what it looks like, it's an ever-changing journey. Even if your best requires retracing some old steps, you must take advantage of the Conflict Crossroads to possess the right tools at the right time. What I mean by this is that Conflict Crossroads are part of what prepares you to effectively deal with your next step.

Again, this is not to say that staying put is bad, or that being comfortable is evil, or that the status quo is wrong. What I will say, however, is that if discovering and walking in your personal best is your ultimate mission in life, then what do you expect to gain by standing still at Conflict Crossroads? Nothing!

Do you imagine that if you linger there at the intersection between complacency and possibility long enough, your best will get impatient and come looking for you? Do you think it will double back and try a fly-by, hoping to catch you even though you didn't go looking for it? *No!*

Your best is like a meal when you're hungry—it's not going to shop for itself, cook itself, plate itself, crawl into your mouth, and chew itself. You've got to put forth a little effort (okay, a lot of effort), if you want to feed your belly and satisfy that craving that made you hungry in the first place.

Even a fast-food meal means you have to get in the car, bring money, and drive through someplace. Even delivery means you have to make a choice, pick up the phone—or nowadays click a mouse—go to the door, pay someone, and put the meal on the table. No hunger ever gets satisfied without effort.

Why should your best be any different? Remember, you've already committed to giving your best so you can receive your best. That includes crossroads. Step hard or go home!

Running on Empty

The real question some of us have to ask ourselves as we approach these Conflict Crossroads is, what is the litmus test we use to make the decision we're being forced to deal with? What, in our background, has prepared us to go left or right, north or south? Have we become familiar enough with our own personal road map to be familiar with the direction we need to go? Is our GPS (global positioning system) plugged in, sending us signals to help us choose right over wrong, progress over complacency? Have we put enough on the line to be brave enough to take the steps we need to go where we intend?

Hopefully by this point we've internalized enough from what we've learned in this book that this should be easy—or at least, easier—but if these "decision intersections" were easy they wouldn't be called *Conflict Crossroads.*

The Mystery of Movement: Four Signs You're at Conflict Crossroad

If I'd been paying more attention as a young professional I would've realized that I missed the highway sign reading CONFLICT CROSSROAD, 20 MILES AHEAD. Fortunately—as life has taught me and I've taken the time to learn—when a Conflict Crossroad is approaching, prepare accordingly.

This knowledge is a valuable tool, because knowing a decision intersection is on the way helps you prepare for the ultimate decision itself. By the way, not all decisions—even the big ones—qualify as Conflict Crossroads.

For instance, buying your dream house isn't really a Conflict Crossroad (when you can afford it) because, let's face it, it's your dream house and you have saved to buy it. So where's the conflict in that? Likewise, marrying the man or woman of your dreams—while a huge decision in and of itself—may not classify as a Conflict Crossroad because your love and friendship are so natural, so unique, so tested that there's no conflict. With all these decisions, the person making them never viewed the converse as an option. *No conflict.*

But even small decisions can be Conflict Crossroads. Taking a new job, not exactly war and peace, can have huge repercussions no matter how you choose.

So how can you tell the difference between a simple decision and a major one? Fortunately, there are several clear indicators that let you know whether something is a simple decision or a Conflict Crossroads.

Indicator 1: A Decision Must Be Made

First and foremost, a Conflict Crossroads forces you to realize—a decision MUST be made. You can't move forward or backward until you make a move. At certain times in our lives we have the option to choose. This is why so-called big decisions, like promotions and uprooting your entire life, aren't always Conflict Crossroads.

So let's say you've been an office peon for going on six years now, and life is good. Not great, but good. Your job is fairly easy, your paycheck's pretty fat, you've got a nice place, nice car, not a ton of debt, and even less pressure. But you've been gunning for a management slot in this Fortune 500 company for almost as long as you've had the job.

Well, suddenly your ship comes in. A colleague has retired and your boss offers you the job. Hooray! Right? Well, not exactly. This is a promotion into one of the toughest departments in one of the toughest companies, working for one of the toughest executives in the nation. This woman has written books on management and is notorious for being a harsh and unforgiving taskmaster.

So while the benefits are top-notch (the bump in pay is life-changing), so is the dread you feel at going from your cushy, humdrum existence to a suddenly frantic, demanding world and the expectation that there will definitely be a cruel adjustment period followed by a long-term sense of ramping up to speed. It's what you've been working steadily for your entire career, and everyone who knows you thinks you'd be a fool to turn it down—including yourself.

Self, meet Conflict Crossroads!

So you see, minor decisions—even if there are major stakes involved—don't qualify as Conflict Crossroads because you can still make the choice to decide or not. Conflict Crossroads are "decision intersections" because you have to make the choice if you want to move closer to your dreams.

Indicator 2: No One Can Make the Decision for You

The second indicator of a Conflict Crossroad is that no one can make the decision for you. This isn't something that anyone can to come in and save you from. This is when you're totally alone in determining what the next step will be.

You can still seek the support of those you turn to for counsel: your family, your friends, your colleagues, your mentor. . .hell, your dog if that works for you. But, ultimately, you have to make the decision for yourself.

Some decisions in life are joint ones: where to go on vacation, how to spend that economic stimulus check or tax refund, whether to rent or own. Such decisions can be made by committee. Conflict Crossroads can't.

Unfortunately, the line between simple decisions and life-altering ones at those decision intersections can often seem quite similar. At the end of the day, only you can tell the difference.

Let's say there's a business colleague or a church member who, for whatever reason, is jealous of you. In front of others, they publicly challenge you to a fight. You're thinking, "Really. . .are we not adults?" However, you're forced to answer. "What do I do?" As far as I see it, you have three choices: (a) walk away, (b) stand your ground and only fight if attacked, or (c) decide to be the aggressor and attack him before he attacks you.

So, what's it going to be: your pride or your future? After all, they obviously have nothing to lose by fighting you. (This is probably why he hates you in the first place.)

The question isn't about the other person. The question is: what do *you* have to lose. Think of the repercussions. It's not as simple as sticking up for your honor. It's about making a split-second decision that could have an impact on your entire future. It's at this moment that you stand alone—no boss, spouse, parent or friend is able to step in and make this decision for you.

Indicator 3: A Sacrifice Must Be Made

You will have to sacrifice something. You aren't going to be able to go through a Conflict Crossroad carrying everything you had going into it. Something's going to have to give. Whether it's a relationship, money, job, or simply comfort, you'll have to give something up.

I loved running track. As I said earlier, it was my life for most of my first nineteen years on this planet. I'd been running track longer than I'd not been running track, so it was extremely hard to give up. Yet I knew that serving as Black Student Union president was going to consume all my time and that there was no way I could do both at the same time.

I am one who gives life its all. Most purposeful people do this. So as upset as I was to jettison track from my life, I received a greater reward by the promise of creating change on campus and physically impacting students' lives. Yes, quitting track was a sacrifice, but it didn't kill me, even if it did almost kill my parents!

In crossing that particular Conflict Crossroad I gave up more than just running track. I gave up my scholarship—money—and had to get a loan instead. So I was affected not just physically but financially (those things don't pay themselves back). Even though the reward was twice what it cost me, it still stung a bit.

Such is life in the pursuit of your best. There will be things you're forced to leave behind, to do without, to give up or compromise on. Think of it this way, though. Whether you work in a big, plush office on a lightning-fast desktop, surrounded by perfect lighting and a noise-resistant cubicle, or are cramped with your laptop in a corner booth at some noisy coffee shop, you can still do the same work. Sure, maybe the laptop's slower, the lighting's not so hot, and the people at the next table chew with their mouths open, but you can accomplish the same task without all the bells and whistles of your cushy office. You just have to recognize the change and respond accordingly.

Have you ever seen one of those old movies where the heroes are trying to get away in an old boat or a raggedy biplane powered by propellers? The bad people are chasing them, gaining on them, and the pilot/captain yells at the crew, "We've got to get rid of some of this cargo if we're going to lose them!"

The heroes look at their crates and crates of precious artifacts or family heirlooms or gaudy treasures, shrug, and start tossing them overboard. And suddenly the ship or the prop plane lifts or speeds up and zooms off, leaving the bad people in the dust? That's a little like what going through a really serious Conflict Crossroad feels like—you're going to have to get rid of some dead weight if you're going to move closer to the right destination.

Indicator 4: Receiving the Gift

Finally, you can tell you're at a major decision intersection when you receive something you didn't have before the Conflict Crossroad, be it an opportunity, gift, information, or wisdom.

I remember being in Toledo while toiling away in corporate America working for some finance company and absolutely hating it. I prayed that God would give me a job that would align with my ministry. My prayer was answered when I was offered a job at the national office of the NAACP, headquartered in Baltimore.

Most of you would say, "Hallelujah, so what's he complaining about?" The reality was far from a storybook ending. At the time my fiancée and I were expecting a child. I wanted to create a stable environment for my family and it made no sense to move from Ohio to Maryland at that point in time. Everything favored staying in Ohio. There, at least, I had a stable job, a 401(k), we knew the area, enjoyed our lives, and could count on great health insurance when the baby arrived. So, this move made no sense at all.

Correction: it made no sense to anyone but me. I recognized the opportunity to work for an organization that mattered and I believed going to Maryland would help me make a giant step forward in my life.

That decision was an essential step to becoming who I am today. I didn't know exactly what I'd be doing, but I knew I wouldn't feel as whole and satisfied as I do today had I not done what I did. That's how I knew I was at a genuine Conflict Crossroad. The stint at the NAACP was a gift that launched a new life, one that directed me toward my personal best rather than against it.

The Layover: Letting People Off, Letting People On, and Refueling

Another characteristic of Conflict Crossroads is that they force us to make a decision that doesn't make sense to anyone else. It's those places that normally determine when a road that we've been traveling on with others will soon be a road we're traveling alone.

As you move through a Conflict Crossroad you'll encounter what I call the Layover. The Layover is a period of transition. For those of you who don't travel often, a layover is when the plane lands, a group of people get off the plane, another group gets on, and the crew refuels for the remainder of the trip.

Our Conflict Crossroads require us to make layovers because the decision to go forward is so brave that it will force others to get on and off your plane. Let's face it: not every spouse is going to be up to making the journey with you. They might not want to give up the security of your present job for this "pipe dream" you're following. They might not want to leave behind their family or uproot the kids.

Not every roommate is going to be willing to let you pound the drums all night before your big rehearsal. Not every teammate is going to be willing to work as hard or as long for as little as you are. It doesn't mean they're bad people; just not the right people to be on this particular journey with you. It's time for a layover—let them off the plane and make room for others who are ready to travel.

There are those who will now get on the plane because you've dedicated yourself to a new level of thinking, of operating, and consequently a new type of individual needs to enter your circle. Maybe it's a new relationship with someone who honors and fosters your commitment to finding your personal best. Maybe this is a new roommate who also plays in a band. Maybe it's a new neighbor who can collaborate with you.

There are some of you who'd ask, "Why would I want to make a decision that doesn't make sense to anybody else?" Those of us who've gone through Conflict Crossroads before understand that sometimes you make decisions that make no sense to other people because they've never been where you want to go. These are the decisions that make your purpose your own. These are the decisions that no one else you know—not your friends, not your lover, not your roommate, not your family circle—have ever been required to make. It creates an intimate bond between you and your future, and takes you farther away from what is normal and closer to what you were born to do.

Sometimes a Conflict Crossroad creates separations. It's natural and unnerving.

The Renewal: Letting Go of People, Places, and Things

We do not live in a vacuum; far from it. What affects one often affects many. Oftentimes these Conflict Crossroads put you at odds with the people you care about the most. Maybe you got that dream job and are relocating to the other side of the country. But you'll be leaving your family, who's been relying on you since you graduated from college. What will they do without you there day in and day out?

Maybe your decision to downsize and use the mortgage money to finance your dream company means your wife has to drive an extra twenty minutes to her job from your new, smaller apartment—and your kids have to leave their best friends behind when they switch school districts. Like I said, Conflict Crossroads are rarely easy, and it's wise to remember that you're not the only one affected.

Warning: This does not mean that you turn your back on your family or responsibility, or ignore your friends. It doesn't mean abandoning people simply because they can't quite see the ultimate vision you have for your life. In fact, when you make the right decisions at these Conflict Crossroads, you'll be able to better support your obligations and be wiser, kinder, and more effective with those in your circle. But you have to make the right decisions; you have to be going in the right direction.

The Alchemist, by Paulo Coelho, says when you're walking toward your personal best the universe will conspire toward your success. Conflict Crossroads, turbulent and unpredictable, will always—always—move you drastically closer or drastically farther away from what it is you were intended to do.

Embracing New People, Places, and Things

It's not called a Conflict Crossroad because it's easy and carefree or a "Kum-Bay-Yah" moment. It's a rite of passage, a watershed moment in your life and, as such, requires that you embrace new people, places, and things.

If you were just going to embrace old people, places, and things, it would be called a reunion, not a Conflict Crossroad. While reunions are all well and good, that's not usually where your true purpose is found.

Change is good, but hard—hard because it does mean new people, places, and things. Fortunately, change is much easier to tolerate—even embrace—when we know we're moving toward something and not away from it. Obtaining your personal best is the ultimate carrot dangling at the end of the stick. Knowing that you're moving toward your goal can make these changes as rewarding as they are challenging.

It's all about your attitude. To help you better manage change, here are a quick few tips for embracing it:

- **Invest:** Know that change is a temporary, but necessary investment. Remember that change is inevitable and the only way we can affect change is in how we respond to it.
- **Crest:** No, we're not talking toothpaste here! The "crest" is the top of a wave, that foamy head just before it's ready to break and sizzle onto shore. Think of change as the storm before the calm, and the crest before the wave breaks is what makes everything clear to you. This, too, shall pass, and when it does, you'll begin to see clearly again.
- **Digest:** Give yourself some time to take it all in; digest the change, and see it for what it really is. Moving can be scary. For the first few days in Maryland I felt like I was walking in slow motion. I didn't know where to stop and get a good pizza. All the gas stations were set up differently, and so even getting a candy bar on the way home from work became a frustrating challenge. The streets were narrow and congested. I felt like that sixteen-year-old with a fresh license in his wallet everywhere I went. But I gave it some time, let myself get adjusted, and learned to love my new surroundings. Change can be like that, if only you let it.
- **Rest:** Finally, give it a rest, all of it—your complaining, your upset stomach, your whimpering and whining, your doubt, and your worry. "Flip a switch," as one of my colleagues likes to tell me, and see the positives instead of the negatives. Know that not all change is bad and that all change produces more change. Welcome this aspect and rest easy in the knowledge that you're doing something positive—for a change!

Chapter 11

Solitude: Learn to Stand Alone

Often at workshops, participants ask why they have to go through loneliness to reach their personal best. Experience has shown me that no one completes the journey to his or her personal best without a period of going it alone. This period of solitude is like going into a cave. You're in the world but no longer of it.

For some, this period of seeming isolation will be the result of natural evolution. People who were once part of your loyal tribe no longer share your vision. Or you may need to answer an inner call to prepare for the next level. Either way most of us haven't prepared the kind of lifestyle that supports prolonged solitude.

Stop! Don't be scared and don't punk out before you even start. This chapter explains why your "cave experience" is so necessary, and how to use it as a springboard for reaching your best self. During this crucial time, you will need three things.

First is an *unwavering source of light* that keeps you connected to a clear picture of your destination, because periods of solitude can often make you feel as if you're standing in the dark. It's at this stage more than any other on your journey that you must have an indelible and detailed picture of your best. As with any picture, the closer you get to it, the more details you should be able see. This is not some form of modern art that looks great far off, but when you get close it turns into a dizzying mix of colors and textures. This picture of your best actually glows. Your light is not simply the light at the end of the tunnel that will guide you out of the cave of solitude. It's also the torchlight to help you discover the secret treasures hidden in the darkness. In practical terms, your focus will be on the detailed picture of your best and the thought of being in and taking up residence in that place. Remember, this is a picture of you, in this moment, being your best, not you en route to your best. That's what makes the picture radiate its own special light.

The second thing you need for your cave experience is *food,* meaning information. During this period you need to consume as much information about your destination as possible. You should be reading instead of talking with friends on the phone, or surfing the Internet's vast information buffet in search of clues about your destination. Think of it as the time spent before going on vacation when you're researching where to eat, the must-see areas, the best beaches, or the hottest clubs. Your cave research will prepare you to find your way around a place you've never been to before, which in this case is your personal best life. When you're searching for your best, you must identify what it is that'll feed you. Is it a book on how to be a better parent, or do you need a DVD on building a website? Will you take a business class at the community college, or will you seek counseling for some lingering emotional issue in your life? Your daily food requirement consists of whatever will strengthen you to become your best and give you the power to stay there.

Finally, you need *confidence*. The belief that allowed you to start your journey now must be transformed into a swagger that allows you to walk into new places, even the darkest of caves, with your head held high. Your belief got you here, but now it's not enough. At this point, you must go beyond belief. Confidence is not faith. Confidence is about knowing who you're not, knowing who you are, and knowing who you're getting ready to become. Now you must move beyond who you think you can become to arrive at who you know you are.

If you fail to take these three things—light, food, and confidence—into your cave of solitude, you may not make it out. Although many people are afraid of solitude, it actually provides three things that are essential for reaching your personal best:

- The opportunity to walk alone
- The silence to hear the Universe
- The confidence to walk with freedom

Why You Need a Cave of Solitude

The cave metaphor can help you understand the period of time between all of the work we've discussed in earlier chapters and when you receive confirmation that you've achieved your personal best. This is the crucial point where it can't be about what anybody else says to you or what anyone other than you has done. It can't be about the competence of your team or the mistakes you've learned from. It can't be about any of those things. You have to be in the place where you know who you are, what your personal best vision is, and what you've learned through this process. You've arrived at the place where you and only you, alone, must make the final preparations necessary to occupy and own the place you've been fighting to get to.

To do this—to actually get to this place—you can't be distracted by the noise swirling around you. Many of us never realize how distracting the outside world can be. TV, text messages, e-mails, tweets, IMs (instant messages), iPods, you name it—our society has created enough technology for us to never be alone. Your cave is a refuge where you can hear yourself think, receive new revelation, and strengthen yourself for the next level. There are different ways to end up in a place of solitude, but rest assured sooner or later you'll be there. How you handle it will determine how you finish your personal best journey.

Sometimes, you'll choose solitude: you'll intentionally seek this refuge with the purpose of coming out renewed. Sometimes, it'll be forced upon you, because you're preparing to be set up for something that you don't even realize is coming your way. Thus, there are moments of intentional solitude as well as moments of unplanned or forced solitude. This doesn't mean that solitude is arbitrary. In this case, solitude is a strategic choice, aimed to prepare you for the next evolution of that whole you.

Many of us lack the discipline or focus to plan our own moments of solitude, so God (the universe) creates the opportunity for you. Whether you believe in God, or that the universe controls itself, this is forced solitude, and it's essential if you're going to reach your personal best.

Light is the thing that gives us encouragement. Anyone who's ever watched a prison movie knows that when somebody is put in the hole (solitary confinement), it's dark down there. Sometimes you'll see prisoners crowding up near the bars, because that's where they can see a flicker of light. Often, that flicker of light is a picture of the world outside of the hole that makes the prisoner realize that he or she is still connected to humanity.

When you're in a cave of forced solitude, the people you normally talk to may be too busy to respond. They may not understand what it is you're trying to do or where you're trying to go. They may be focused on their own personal issues. At these times, you may not be invited to as many events as you once were. Your social calendar may be empty. Now, you have to find the motivation to push and encourage yourself forward. Earlier, when you created your vision, it might have been a little bit vague or general. You were just beginning to step out of the mediocrity of your life, to push toward your personal best. You believed that you deserve your best, you jumped off, you developed your strategy, and you put together your team. You've been on this journey long enough now that your vision can no longer be vague. It can no longer be arbitrary. You've gone through enough stops on your map to be closer to your best than ever before. Your Power Notes and journal entries have helped you clarify the picture and how you look in it. You should now be able to say to yourself:

- I clearly know the kind of father I want to be. I've been working out these parenting strategies, and I know what works and what doesn't. My early efforts to reengage with my kids are paying off.

- I know what kind of CEO (or entrepreneur) I want to be. I've made several mistakes, but I've recovered from them and mapped out a new business management strategy.

- I know exactly what kind of spouse I want to be. We've gone through counseling, worked through our mistakes, and prioritized how to be more emotionally available to each other.

You now have a clear picture of where you are and what you want and if you don't, something's wrong. The clear picture is the light you're going to focus on in your cave of solitude. If you don't have a clear picture, you're in the dark.

Seasons of Solitude

Periods of solitude are not something you schedule every day. In fact, the time needed for solitude varies from person to person. For some, it may be a season. For others, it might be several weeks. For still others, it might be a completely uninterrupted weekend. For example, Jack is a successful entrepreneur who has a lot of flexibility with his schedule. He goes away by himself to a very secluded monastery in the mountains of West Virginia for twenty days straight, every year. He spends his time there in almost total silence and focuses on what he wants to do during the year ahead, and what parts of his life he wants to improve to be his personal best.

Most of us don't have the discipline or the luxury to take twenty days a year, but we can begin to schedule periods of solitude without ever leaving the house. That doesn't mean you separate yourself from your family (because you still have a responsibility to them), but it does mean you cut down on unnecessary conversations with friends, stop watching recreational television, stay off of the Internet, and don't participate in social events. By regularly separating yourself from your normal world and interactions, you give yourself the gift of time. For some, it might be every few months, for others it might be once a year. Take the time you need so you can focus in a real way on where you are and where you're going and silence all the noise around you to strengthen yourself for the journey ahead.

My friend James has an interesting cycle that occurs about every three or four years: he changes jobs at the tail end of one of his solitude seasons. His solitude always begins with a sense of disconnect with his work or personal life. He finds himself thinking, "I no longer feel the genuine satisfaction that I once got from work. This environment is no longer productive for me." For example, when he left the corporate world to become an entrepreneur, it wasn't because of dissatisfaction at work; it was as a result of challenges at home, which made him feel that something was wrong with him. James went into his cave. He stopped talking to friends, and gave himself extra time for meditation and contemplation. He asked himself, "Where am I not right now, where do I need to be right now, and what's getting in the way of that?"

James's bosses were pressing him to put in extra hours and to complete assignments that weren't part of his job description. He was stressing out regularly, and bringing that energy home. As he began to think about what he needed to do differently, he realized his wife was great and his kids were great. He realized that the source of his discomfort was his *job*. It was during a moment of solitude that he looked at the picture of who he wanted to be, and said to himself, "I'm doing all these negative things at home, but the problem lies at work." That was the springboard for his entrepreneurial venture and real change.

Food for the Journey

This cave of solitude is not barren. It is a place that allows you the time and quiet focus to take in new sources of food that consist of things that will sustain you now and later. Food for the journey is what you consume that will strengthen you intellectually, physically, or emotionally—the fortifying resources you can access in solitude. Getting to your personal best is not about a weekend visit. Getting to your personal best is the place that you're moving to, and if you don't have everything it takes to be able to move and stay there, a weekend visit isn't going to do you much good.

My brother, Jamon, began training to run in the New York City Marathon. Anybody who prepares for a marathon knows there's no way you can maintain the life you had before, because you can't eat the same way you used to, the workouts you must do are ridiculously intense, your social life and even your sleeping patterns have to shift because you're preparing your body for this incredible exertion. The same is true on your journey to your personal best: you need to lead many aspects of your life differently, to prepare yourself for your destination.

After all, there's nothing worse than seeing somebody elevated to a place she or he is not prepared for. For example, Brian constantly talked about wanting to be on television. He had a crazy work ethic. He worked hard. He hustled. He networked incredibly well. He was well spoken, and impressed everyone who heard him. However, Brian never studied. He never studied the news or the issues that he said he cared about. He was a smart man, but he didn't have the wealth of knowledge required to be a good TV commentator. Still, he wanted to be on TV.

Brian was very passionate about education. He knew enough to talk about the disparities in secondary education, what Head Start used to be and why it was important, and the lack of access to financial resources for college education. As a result, a local station that was looking for someone to do some cable access shows invited Brian to be a guest, as a springboard to other opportunities.

The topic of the show was, of course, education. Brian was paired with a person with conservative views on school choice and education policy. During the interview, it quickly became clear that Brian's information was outdated and disconnected from relevant current policy. Naturally, his opponent ripped him to shreds because Brian hadn't fed himself with what he needed to succeed in presenting his position. There are times when people get opportunities, but they aren't prepared because they didn't fortify themselves with the food they needed to be strong.

Unfortunately, Brian never appeared on television again. He realized his mistake, but you aren't always given another chance, which is why when you get a chance, you have to be prepared.

What good is it to go through all of the preparation for your journey, building a team that can help you, giving your all, creating your strategy, and learning from your mistakes, only to arrive at your destination and find yourself ultimately unprepared, empty of the things you need to stay there once you get there?

Confidence vs. Arrogance

Brian had a vision, but he didn't really have confidence. Confidence is not about what you think you can do. It's about what you know you can do. All the belief that you've manifested throughout the personal best process allows you to say:

...This isn't what I think I can do.
...This isn't what I have the capacity to do.
...This isn't what I have the vision to do.
...Because I went through this process, I *know* I can do this.
...I know I have my strategy in place.
...I know I have scheduled moments of solitude to remind myself of what I need to do.
...I know that I've begun the process of walking these things out.
...I know that I've dealt with my past mistakes,
...I'm no longer imprisoned by them.
...I know that I'm free and able to move forward.
...Because I know these things, I'm no longer a conventional caterpillar of mediocrity filled with dissatisfaction.
...I know that when I'm ready I'll shed this cocoon, because I'm now a butterfly able to express my very best.

My friend, Kevin Coburn from Toledo, Ohio, is a great example of this stage of development. His story could be the plot for an after-school special. Kevin grew up in Cleveland. When in high school, after his parents divorced, he worked at an after-school job. Unlike other kids who had part-time jobs, Kevin wasn't working to have money for cassette tapes (the way we bought music back then!) or so he could go to the movies or out on a date. Instead, Kevin was working because, if he did not, his mother wouldn't have been able to pay the rent or put food on the table. Kevin worked thirty hours a week at a grocery store while still in high school!

He has often talked about the day a guidance counselor from his school came into his store and asked him, "Don't you go to Cleveland Heights High School? I come in here all the time, and every time I come in, you're here." When Kevin answered that he was still in school, the counselor asked him how many hours a week he worked. Kevin told him. Astounded, the counselor asked him, "When do you study?" Kevin answered that he didn't have time to study.

The guidance counselor was somewhat surprised. "Your grades aren't bad. Do you realize what you could do if you took time to study?" Kevin explained that he couldn't take time to study because he had to help his mother support their family. The counselor persisted. "Aren't you thinking about college?" to which Kevin replied, "I'm not thinking about college. I'm going to go get a full-time job here to help my mom."

The counselor refused to let it go at that. Instead, he told Kevin about financial aid and other types of assistance for college that Kevin had never heard about. Simply as a result of this guidance counselor's advice and interest in him, Kevin began to believe that maybe he could do something more with his life than simply work in a grocery store. He began to see that maybe there is a best Kevin who could be a college graduate and not the manager of a grocery store. He dared to begin a new journey. He applied for financial aid, which enabled him to go to school, and it took a financial burden off his mother.

Kevin went through all the processes laid out in this book: he selected a major, focused on his schoolwork, and began to build his strategy and team. He joined a fraternity and got involved in campus organizations. He made mistakes, as we all do, but did not wallow in them. Instead, he pushed himself past them, and, at the same time, mentored other young black men at the University of Toledo—including me.

He graduated, then went on to get his master's in education. At that point, Kevin went through the process of creating a new vision of the person he could be, which went something like, "I can simply teach or I can change the world." Kevin began to see himself working with young people, especially disadvantaged young people, and helping them to change their perspective on life, the way his guidance counselor helped him change his perspective on his life.

Kevin began to focus on how he could do that. He decided to create a group-home like environment for young boys who didn't have a place to live or who had been removed from their homes, for whatever reason. Some people told him he was crazy, and some even disconnected from him, leaving him out there all by himself. That was when Kevin went into his cave of solitude.

Undeterred, Kevin researched and researched and researched. He read everything he could get his hands on. He wrote, both to get out all the thoughts and experiences he had, and to organize them into a curriculum of sorts. Finally, he developed a curriculum and processes. When he came out of this moment of solitude, the picture of what he wanted to do was bigger than when he'd gone into it. That alone time allowed him to tailor and focus his vision.

Eventually, Kevin and his partners were able to get an old school building, which they converted into a center for disenfranchised young men—kids who might otherwise have been put in juvenile detention centers. Kevin's dream provided them with a residence where they could be safe, as well as an educational environment where they could learn.

Fast forward several years: Kevin has now created a curriculum that's connected with the city schools in Toledo and, from his program alone, has reduced the suspension and arrest rate of the same population of young men by 30%–40%.

Kevin went through this cocoon process to separate himself from the non-believers. He consciously went into the cave where he could see the light and develop his vision. In this place, he was able to feed himself information through reading, research, and writing. He emerged from the cocoon with the confidence that he could create something that hadn't existed before, which could change the lives of young people in his city. By the way, this school still exists, and Kevin still runs it. Moreover, he is currently working on having his curriculum adopted throughout the entire Toledo school system.

Aloneness Is Not Loneliness

There is a difference between being alone and being lonely. When you're in a place of solitude, you're continually building toward your best. You're motivated and focused, and acknowledge that this period is a finite amount of time that will ultimately elevate you. By contrast, when you're spiraling downward or depressed, you're unable to build. Depression keeps you in a place where you don't want to get out of bed. You're just going through the motions, immobilized in many areas of your life.

The difference is clear. When you're in a place of solitude, and you find that you're less and less motivated, that it's difficult to get anything done, and you're not thinking positively, then it's time to recognize that the place you're in isn't solitude—it's depression. I know people who have dealt with depression—people who've been able to reach success in one area, even though they're barely functioning in other areas of their life.

If you're intentionally separating yourself from other people, not so you can focus on what you're doing, but because you just don't want to talk to or be around anybody, it's an indication that you're either spiraling down into or already are in a place of depression. At that point, you need to seek help.

Intentional vs. Forced Solitude

Truly intentional or forced moments of solitude are about cocooning yourself to metamorphose into your best. It's not about isolating yourself to hide from whatever it is you need to deal with.

When you go through an intentional period of solitude, it's helpful at the outset to identify how long you're going to stay there because you don't want to get stuck in a rut.

You don't want to put yourself in a place where you're indefinitely in a cave and don't know how to escape. Sometimes people have unrealistic expectations, such as, "I'm going to stay in the cave until I reach this point," instead of getting as much out of those moments of solitude as you can for a finite amount of time. At the end of your time in the cave, you should realize that you're going to continue to grow, feed yourself, and hone your vision even after you come out of the cave. Being in the cave is just an isolated moment that gives you the ability to focus and grow stronger.

That's why it's so important to set a time limit before you start, whether it's seven days, two weeks, or an entire month. However, I don't recommend that intentional solitude last longer than a month, because then you may isolate yourself.

There may be times when you have to tell your friends, family, and others who care about you that you need some time alone to focus on things. You may even decide to share some of those things with them. This lets the people in your life know that, although you may not be talking with them regularly, you're still healthy and moving forward. This may seem cumbersome, but it helps other people in your life become more comfortable about your cocooning, when they might otherwise think you're depressed instead of in a place of growth.

It's important to remember that at no point should you feel as if you're going to come out of the cave perfect. You're not separating yourself to become a "best superhero," but taking a moment of solitude to strengthen yourself in some specific areas, to do things you couldn't do before you entered the cave. You don't have to know everything, or do everything, or be ready for everything. When a caterpillar cocoons itself, it doesn't do so in an effort to become invincible. It creates the cocoon so that it can transform itself into a butterfly, the next stage in its metamorphosis to its best self-expression.

Forced solitude is harder to deal with than intentional solitude. Many of us, while on the journey, may find that, because we've changed who we want to be and how we do things, that the people around us are no longer headed in the same direction. Because you didn't plan to be by yourself, forced solitude can leave you a bit discombobulated, disconnected, and even confused about how to deal with being by yourself and without the friends who've stopped calling.

Eric was an average kid of Chinese descent growing up in a very mixed suburb outside of Oakland, California. The boys he ran with were second- and third-generation Chinese-Americans, kids who pretty much embraced the hip-hop subculture. They were suburban kids trying to live out ghetto fantasies. They created their own little crew that they called a "gang," fought other crews, and got into a bunch of trouble. It was nothing criminal, just rambunctious kid stuff that kept getting them into trouble.

One summer, Eric spent a couple of weeks in Los Angeles with his older brother Frank, who went to UCLA. Frank was involved in some very positive things. He was a good student, was trying to start his own business and had a great girlfriend. All his friends we're trying to make something out of their lives. Bottom line: Frank was a very positive role model.

Although Frank was three years older than Eric, he'd been involved in the same kind of trouble as Eric when he was in high school. When Eric saw how his brother's life had changed—and how he was succeeding in college, work, and life in general—Eric realized that he was wasting time with his crew. Frank showed Eric that the stuff he was doing wasn't going to take him anywhere.

When Eric returned home, he started to look at his life differently, and started to figure out what he wanted to do with his life. He set his sights on Boston College, Harvard, or Princeton. He always had good grades even when he was hanging with his boys, but he knew that if he were arrested for fighting or beating someone up or even disturbing the peace, that might prevent him from getting into a top college. Hanging out on the street wouldn't leave him any time for the extracurricular activities that counted on college applications. Once he understood where he wanted to go, Eric started flipping the script.

There was a hip-hop club at his school, where some folks from the community were teaching people how to DJ. Eric loved music, and also had an interest in computers, so he joined a group where he could learn new graphics programs that allowed him to create digital graffiti and all kinds of cool multi-media presentations.

Of course, the guys that he'd been running with were pissed off. They confronted him and asked who he thought he was with all this new stuff. Eric never said, "I don't want to hang with you anymore." He didn't set out to make new friends. But when he started doing things differently, none of his old crew called him. When his name showed up on their caller IDs, they didn't answer the phone. Eric began to question himself, "What the hell is going on? What did I do wrong? Why am I in this place?"

Forced moments of solitude make us examine our lives and ask, "Does the life that I'm in right now, the things I'm doing right now, the friends I have right now, fit with where I'm getting ready to go?"

Being your best is not a one-time event, and then you're done. It's a way of life, operating, and being. There's a level of accountability and consistency that's necessary to not only get to the place you want to be but, as I have said, *stay there*! Forced solitude may put you in a position to say, "Wait a minute. I'm accountable. I have to be able to tailor this vision, create this light, and see specifically what I want to do. I have to feed myself those things that I need to exist in a new space where I've never been before. These experiences will give me the confidence to walk out and establish new relationships, create new friendships, and challenge old ones. Confidence will help me sustain my personal best, instead of settling for the person I used to be."

Recognize That Forced Solitude Is a Positive

Forced solitude puts us in a position to make ourselves ask important questions. Therefore, people in forced solitude have to remember three things.

First, once you realize you're in a place of forced solitude, recognize that it's not a bad or negative place, and that you didn't do anything wrong. There's nothing inherently flawed about you. This is simply a reflection of you trying to be your best.

Avoid the psychological stress that comes from feeling guilty—the false notion that something is wrong with you because the people who used to be around you may no longer want to stay around you. Remember, there's nothing wrong with you. Face this from the outset or you'll never use your forced solitude productively.

G is two years out of undergraduate school and in a training program at a major Fortune 500 company. He's certain that, once he completes his training program, he'll be set professionally and on track for an executive position. The problem that he's facing is personal. He's been in a cycle of deceptive and manipulative relationships with women, but now he's decided, "I don't want to do this anymore. I want to change." Part of his new conviction grew out of personal morality, part came from religious conviction. Nonetheless, having reached this conclusion, G is beginning to regard his relationships quite differently.

The challenge facing G is that the women he's involved with aren't really interested in a guy who doesn't want to have sex, go out and party, or get drunk. So after a while, G has found himself increasingly alone. The women he used to date are no longer interested, and he hasn't found any new circles to operate in. Understandably, G has become very lonely.

In this forced solitude, there should be a moment when he is able to say, "This is where I need to be. Here's how I need to do this. This is my vision of the type of man I want to be, with respect to women. Here's the kind of food I want to feed myself, which could be bible verses or women who want different things." With that understanding, G should achieve the confidence to know that he can be that kind of person. Unfortunately G said to himself, "I don't need to be doing this. I'm young. I can do this later. Now, I should be partying and having a good time. I'm making too big a deal of this, because nobody around me gets what I'm trying to do anyway." G demonized himself because the people around him couldn't handle it. If he'd been able to understand that his forced solitude was not a bad thing, but rather a natural reflection of his decision to do better, he might have been able to stay in his cave for a moment. He might have been able to begin to feed himself the food necessary to encourage and sustain his change. Then he could have developed the genuine confidence to come out of the cave and use that energy to establish new kinds of relationships.

Because he didn't do that, G spent another six months in a very dysfunctional and dissatisfying mode. Six months later, G realized that he couldn't settle for this anymore.

Both Eric and G went through the process of taking a stand for who they were, and both discovered that their personal best was not consistent with their old friendships. Each had to make a choice.

Similarly, if you've said, "This is not who I want to be" and your friends reject you, you have to have a really hard conversation with yourself. If your friends abandon you for becoming a different person, they may no longer be in the same place as you. Others may stick by you nonetheless and agree to find new interests to pursue when they're with you. As friends, we have the ability to mentor or minister to each other.

Just because some friends appear to abandon you doesn't mean they don't care about you. It doesn't mean that if you're in real trouble and really in a crunch that you can't call on them. It just means they aren't ready to walk on the road that you're ready to walk on. Being around you is sometimes uncomfortable because it forces them to see what they aren't willing to do. Therefore, this isn't a place where you say, "I have to abandon all my friends," or "If I change, all my friends will abandon me, and I better get used to it." This is simply a time and place where you have to recalibrate.

There's no doubt that this process of pushing for your personal best will challenge some relationships. Forced solitude is a manifestation of that growth curve. This is a time, more than ever, that you need to be encouraged—what you're doing is right, and one of two things will happen. Either those friends who don't get what you're doing will at some point be inspired by your focus, or there'll be a necessary separation that gives you the freedom to move forward.

Recently I spoke at the University of Michigan. My speech was about the current state of leadership in America, and how Barack Obama's presidency has made some people lazy, because they think he's the messiah and that he can, and will, fix everything that's bad. What I raised was how to challenge that notion.

After the lecture, a young professional, who'd graduated from college two years earlier, engaged me. He told me how he's been pushing to change the destiny of his family, because he's the fist college graduate. No one in his family had ever owned a business before, and he's already on his entrepreneurial track. Moreover, nobody in his family was married: everyone—grandparents, parents, aunts, uncles—who'd been married had gotten divorced. Yet he was engaged, and preparing to be the kind of husband and father who had never existed in his family.

He said that when he started on this road, "My boys, who used to hang out with me, were not with it. They said, 'You want to be this college boy, and you think you're smart, and you think you're better than us, so go ahead and do your thing.'" The people he'd come up with had turned their back on him, but he remained focused. He didn't go home as much. He focused his energy at school and created some new relationships. Whenever he went home, he talked to his old friends, and they talked to him, but they were never as close as they had been.

"Jeff, I realized at a certain point, they just couldn't see what I saw," he said. "And because they can't see what I can see, they can't respond as I responded."

Most of us do what we know or what we've been taught or what we've seen somewhere. This guy's friends didn't see what he saw. They didn't see his desire to be better, his desire to create something new. Therefore, they couldn't respond.

He told me he'd gone home about three weeks before we met, and had run into one of his friends on the street who'd heard he was engaged.

"Man, congratulations. I heard you were getting married," his old friend said. "I hear that you're starting your business. You know when you started talking about you was going to flip the script and do all of this stuff, I didn't really feel you. But I see that it worked for you. I'm going through some difficult times right now. Everything I thought I was supposed to be doing isn't what I'm supposed to be doing, and you've really been an inspiration to me. I just felt like I needed to tell you that, because I kind of played you, back in the day. I just want to let you know that you were right. I got my GED, and I'm enrolling at community college."

Many of us have to go through the unfortunate process of disconnecting from people that we've come up with, or people we care about. But we have to realize that by being strong in those times, we not only redirect our lives, we may ultimately help redirect our friends' lives as well.

Embrace the Opportunity

The second thing people in forced solitude must do is embrace the opportunity, which means that, although it might not be what you'd have choreographed for yourself, you should still take this moment and use the time for your benefit. How many times do people say, "I wish I had more time. I wish I had more time to do this, I wish I had more time focus on that. I wish I didn't have so many things pulling at me." Then when they get that time, they think it's bad.

Take this opportunity to understand that where you are isn't where you have to be.

Know That Things Will Change

Once you've understood that forced solitude isn't a bad thing, once you've confirmed that nothing's wrong with you and you've taken advantage of the opportunity to use this time to feed yourself, you have to forecast your exit. This solitude was unplanned, and you can't stay in it forever. Ask yourself, "How am I going to use this time, and when am I going to end it?"

Regardless of the type of solitude you find yourself in, remember that this is a very important and critical moment in your process. The focus, strength, and confidence that can emerge from this period in the cave may surprise even you. Embrace the moment, walk it out, and emerge from your cave closer to your best than you've ever been in your life.

PART IV

LIVING YOUR BEST

Confirmation

Confirmation is that moment, event, or opportunity that signifies that all the work you've done was worth it. It's a revelation that signifies that you've reached the place you've been working toward. It's the answer to the question, "How will I know when I've arrived?"

Sometimes your confirmation will resemble an athlete breaking the tape at the finish line of an Olympic marathon. There's no doubt that you've just crossed over to your personal best. Sometimes, however, you may be like the slaves in Texas who celebrated Juneteenth because they didn't know that slavery was over, so while they were "officially" free they needed actual confirmation to walk in their freedom. No matter how your confirmation happens, it's important that you acknowledge it so that your actions begin to shift from getting there to staying there.

Different people realize that they've reached their personal best in different ways. For some, their confirmation came with the promotion that arrived the same month as the best wedding anniversary they've ever had. For others, their confirmation came on the day they realized that the personal issues that had stressed them out for the last three years were no longer points of anxiety. For still others, the confirmation was much more subtle, and it wasn't until they took a moment to breathe that they realized that their lives were different.

You must understand the fact that there will not be a single confirmation moment. Instead, these moments will happen regularly when you're on the journey to your personal best to remind you that you're there. You'll inevitably learn to look for these moments and treasure them, as they'll be continuous affirmations that you're in the right place, your best place.

Self-Confirmation

In this chapter, we'll force — yes, force — you to go through a self-confirmation process. There's a familiar bible story that in many ways encapsulates the notion of confirmation after isolation. The basics of the story are that, after fasting alone for forty days and nights, Jesus is confronted by Satan, and is tempted to renounce God and proclaim his own power. Jesus simply responds with the Word of God that he'd been meditating on during his fast. He didn't get angry, he didn't get frustrated, nor did he give in. Instead, he became a reflection of the light (which was the detailed vision of his best), the food (which was the "Word of God" that he consumed), and the confidence that he was who he was and not who Satan told him to be. He was walking in his best.

You, too, will be tested not long after you leave your cave of solitude. How you handle that test is your confirmation. It's uncomfortable for most people (whether you're Christian or not) to compare themselves to Jesus, so as we proceed, I'll highlight the confirmation stories of mortals.

Self-confirmation is your recognition that you've made it to that place, that destination toward which you were heading. It's similar to a long-distance drive from Ohio to Atlanta. You don't necessarily get confirmation that you've passed the Georgia state line, perhaps because you missed the sign, but when you begin to notice that the exit number signs have changed, and your exit is ahead then you have absolute confirmation that you've arrived.

Confirmation that you've arrived at your destination is important because this is the moment when you move from being on your journey to actually arriving at your destination and to creating your system for staying there. This is the moment to take time to celebrate all of the work you've done. You've pushed yourself, challenged yourself, and modified yourself. Therefore, you need to take a moment to celebrate the confirmation that you've made it. All the work you've done has actually manifested through the personal best that you envisioned.

Xavier, for instance, was a perpetual cheater. He invented new ways to cheat: he typically dated four, five, six women at a time in three or four different states. He had an amazing system for communicating with all of them and for making each one think that they were the only one in his life. Because his job required him to travel a lot to several cities each week, none of his women expected to see him frequently.

Xavier enjoyed having many women in his life. He didn't want monotony; he wanted variety. He couldn't be honest with any of his women, because the women he dated wouldn't tolerate an "open" relationship. Each one thought she was in a monogamous partnership.

One day, Xavier met a woman whom he fell for, in a completely unexpected way. He told me that he really liked this girl, and had no concept of how to get involved with her the right way. He explained that everything in him was about being a player. He didn't even know how to be honest or monogamous. Xavier said that he wanted me to help him rediscover the person that he was, or show him how to be the person that he wanted to be in the relationship.

I recommended some strategies for first disconnecting himself from the other women he'd been dating. The requirement was being honest enough to tell them the truth: "I met a woman I really care about, and I want to start a relationship with her, and I can't do that and stay in a relationship with you." Mentally, this was his biggest challenge, because his whole MO (*modus operandi*) had been to lie, which he justified by saying he wanted to avoid hurting anyone's feelings. Xavier had never lived by the philosophy of "Let me be honest so that I can respect the women in my life." Ending his relationships with the other women in his life was relatively easy. All it took was a single phone call and a few uncomfortable meetings, during which he had to deal with each woman's reactions and range of emotions, but then he was off the hook.

What was truly difficult for Xavier was being in a monogamous relationship. How would he talk to and engage other women? Now he didn't know how to interact with new women he met. He admitted that his flirtatious seduction act — getting business cards and phone numbers, finding reasons to call or meet a woman — was his hookup methodology. How he defined himself was the most difficult part to shed.

I suggested that when he met new women that he should stop thinking of them as potential dates, or girlfriends, or sex partners.

"Yeah right! What if they are fine women and what if they come on to me?" he defended.

"The first thing is that you have to be more distant than you may want to be in the beginning. That old charming guy attracts more attention than you may be able to handle the first week of you being this new guy. And if you get weak and get a number or a card when you're in a "mack mode relapse," just throw it away when you leave the event. More important, and even more difficult than that (some of my guy friends are reading ..."there's more?!"), I told him he needed to be honest with the new woman he was dating and let her know what he was trying to work through as a boyfriend, and what some of his weaknesses were.

To which Xavier responded, "Now I gotta be a bitch, too." Sharing his feelings and weaknesses was a bit too much of an Oprah moment for Xavier. I told him that intense changes called for intense tactics.

Although his intentions were good, actually being monogamous and honest was a huge challenge for him. Several weeks into this process, Xavier went on vacation to the

Caribbean islands with some of his boys, and two of them put together an incredible party, to which they invited several beautiful women. Vacations in a foreign country seem to promote weekend romances. Jason, a mutual friend on the trip, told me that one of the most gorgeous women he'd ever seen approached Xavier at the party, and said she "wanted to make sure he had a good time this weekend."

Xavier told me the confirmation that he had become an honest, monogamous boyfriend didn't come when he spent ten minutes talking about everything except hooking up, or even when he told this beautiful woman that he was in a relationship, and that cheating was not what he wanted to do. Instead, his confirmation came 10 minutes later, shortly after this beautiful woman walked away.

He sat there for a moment and thought about his girlfriend. He said to himself, "Damn, I'm whipped!" A remark that would have normally set him into automatic prowl mode had been disconnected. That was when he realized, "I've arrived. I am here." That was Xavier's moment of confirmation. Not when he sent the island beauty away, but after. He hadn't thought to himself, "Why did I send her away?" or "Maybe I'll hook up with her later," or "I'm not going out like a punk." He sent her away, and he thought about his new girlfriend—something he'd never done before—and he understood that he'd actually reached the destination he'd been headed toward. Now all he had to do was figure out how to stay there.

Celebrate Your Achievements

In addition to the self-confirmation process, where you acknowledge that you've achieved your vision and reached your destination, you also need to celebrate what you've achieved. For example, Ella, who graduated from Duke Law School at the top of her class, passed the New York Bar exam on her first try and landed a great job with a prestigious law firm.

Ella's immediate goal was to distinguish herself from the other associates in this large firm so that she could eventually get on track to make partner, which is a long-term goal. Anybody who knows the legal field knows new associates work eighty to ninety hours a week just to remain on par, let alone to distinguish themselves from their co-workers. Ella was enmeshed in the standard grind that consumes all young associates, but she understood that her success would require more than working her cases. If she wanted to distinguish herself, especially as a female associate, from her 13 male associates, she'd not only have to work harder than everyone else but also create politically savvy relationships. She knew her bosses were not going to invite her out for a drink, or to a basketball or hockey game, or to play golf, because they'd assume that her interests (as a woman) would be different from theirs. Moreover, these partners were such hard-nosed individuals that they either pretended they didn't know the names of any of the new associates or wouldn't even acknowledge them.

Ella needed a way to connect with her bosses. She decided to profile each partner in the firm and discover what they were interested in—not only the routine things (like whether they played golf, or what city they were from, or what their favorite cigar or drink was), but the nuances. One partner had a passion for the theater; another was a baseball memorabilia fanatic. So even in the midst of her working eighty to ninety hours a week, Ella found ways to thank the partners for involving her in some of the more interesting work, while letting them know she'd been paying attention to their interests. When a partner gave her a new case or introduced her to a potential client, she expressed her gratitude by saying something like, "I was at a flea market this weekend, and I came across this vintage baseball card I thought you might like." Or "I have a friend who works in the theater, and he comp'd me these tickets. I thought you might like to see this new show."

Ella had no idea if any of them had even noticed her work, or her thoughtfulness, or anything about her.

Then one night, Ella was leaving the office very late. It was about 10 PM, and she was one of the last people to leave work. She was turning out the light in her office when one of the partners returned, after having attended an evening event, to pick up something from his office. As she was leaving, she looked at her watch, and the partner noticed and said, "Ella, this is an early night for you, huh?" She said, "Excuse me?" and he said, "I know you normally put in even later hours than this, so enjoy what's left of your evening. You deserve it." While this may seem to some people like a very small passing comment, Ella realized that this acknowledgment meant that this partner knew the hours she was putting in — and that those long hours of hard work weren't meaningless. Most important, his last remark was recognition that she was doing good work and was valued by the company.

This was a confirmation moment for Ella. That recognition, however, didn't mean that this was a moment for Ella to celebrate and say, "Yes, I have made it. Now I can stop working so hard." Instead, this was a moment for Ella to say, "I made it to this point. Now, how do I stay here? How do I continue to acknowledge the partners? How do I continue to do good work? How do I continue to stay in this space that got me to the place where the partners who I wanted to see me as valuable have not only seen me as valuable, but acknowledged that they see me as valuable?"

Ella left the office, went home, and opened a bottle of wine she'd been saving for a special occasion. Nobody else was there, and she didn't call anybody. She just popped open that bottle of vintage Shiraz, sat down with her favorite artisan cheese, and toasted herself. The celebration is really the acknowledgment that you've arrived.

Some people celebrate too long; others don't celebrate enough. Those who celebrate too long believe that, because they received confirmation, they can now celebrate and get comfortable. You simply can't because when you're comfortable, you stop striving. You stop having that hunger and focus that pushed you past mediocrity. You stop fighting for the things that you gave so much of yourself to achieve. You stop following the positive patterns you created. You stop refining your vision. You stop putting those dates and reminders into your BlackBerry and using your journey journal or Power Notes to continue to assess how you're doing. It's as if the people who celebrate too long feel that the fact they've arrived is now enough. Well it isn't, and the longer you stay in that place, the faster you'll find yourself back where you started.

If you're one of those people who do that, you need to acknowledge the fact that you got where you wanted to go. You have to celebrate the fact that you were diligent. You have to pat yourself on the back for the fact that you kept those notes in your BlackBerry or wrote in your journal or Power Notes every week, if not every other day. But you can't let that acknowledgment (or your celebration of it) get in the way of your consistent, day-in and day-out work toward your personal best.

There are ways to celebrate that don't go too far, including going out with your significant other or taking yourself out alone. In fact, I often recommend that people learn to celebrate by themselves, rather than having someone take them out or going out with friends. Select your favorite restaurant, and say, "I'm going to celebrate myself tonight, order my favorite meal, and sit with myself and celebrate my achievement." You can even say, "I'm going to treat myself to that movie I really want to see or that cigar I love so much," or "I'm going to spend the day at my favorite museum," or "I'm not going to work, and I'm not going to write in my journal. I'm going to celebrate this confirmation, and enjoy time with myself doing something I love."

Your personal best is really about the whole you, and if you need somebody else to celebrate it for you, or if you have to be with somebody to do it, how valuable really is it to you? Big up yourself, give yourself a high-five in the mirror and send yourself some flowers. Again, this can be something as small as taking yourself out to dinner for your favorite meal, or just going home, cracking open a beer, and watching your favorite TV show without thinking about anything else for the night. The celebration is not supposed to be, "I'm going to fly off to Paris for the weekend." It's simply taking one day to say, "I did it. I did what I said I was going to do. I made it. I deserve a treat." It's a formal acknowledgment.

On the flip side, there are those who don't celebrate long enough. Such people are afraid to celebrate, because they're afraid that if they acknowledge their achievement too much, it'll be taken away from them. They're afraid that what they've accomplished isn't real or lasting. They're waiting for the bottom to drop out. That's dangerous, too, because such people don't give themselves the opportunity to celebrate. Instead, they work themselves into the ground and have unrealistic expectations of themselves, which destine them for burnout.

I'm a great example of that. From the time I started my professional career at the NAACP, I was busting my behind. I was working as hard as I could. After being there for a year, I was promoted from National Youth Council Coordinator to Assistant Director of Programs. Four months later, I was elevated from Assistant Director of Programs to National Youth Director, a senior staff position at the NAACP. In only two-and-a-half years, I was making three times what I was making when I started there, held a senior staff position, and I had traveled the country representing the NAACP. During those entire three-and-a-half years, I never took a vacation day. Not a single one. I never took a break from work, nothing. I told myself, "I love my job. I love what I'm doing. I'm being promoted. I'm being elevated." I felt I didn't need to take time off, and I didn't want to take time off.

There were many periods of confirmations, promoted to Assistant Director of Programs, elevated to National Youth Director, receiving raises, but I never took the time to celebrate them. The only thing I thought was, "What's next?" I never took those momentary opportunities to celebrate what I'd accomplished, or the success of the program we developed, or the partnership we pulled off. I never said, "I'm pleased with myself and now I have to celebrate this place." Instead, I concentrated on how I was going to make the next move. I never said, Let me at least take the day off and drive down to the Eastern Shore of Maryland, let alone take a vacation.

After three-and-a-half years, I was so stressed that I got to a point where I didn't want to work. I knew I had to work, and I was trying to create opportunities, but I was fatigued. My mind was fatigued. My body was fatigued. I was always tired. I don't think I'd ever acknowledged myself well enough to make me feel good about what I'd done. I'd created this myth that humble people don't celebrate themselves, which is absurd. Humble people aren't ostentatious; they don't put an ad in the paper that they were promoted. They don't buy themselves a fabulous piece of jewelry, or a new house, or a new piece of furniture—none of that is necessary. But you do need to acknowledge and celebrate that the work you set out to do these weeks, these months, or even a year ago, has happened.

I only realized how exhausted I was after I left the NAACP, when I was beating myself up in New York, trying to get my new business off the ground, and things weren't going well. Until that moment, I thought I'd left the NAACP because I simply didn't want to be there anymore. It was only at that moment in New York that I said to myself, "I never celebrated what I did there, ever. I never patted myself on the back. Instead, I beat myself up so much that I never enjoyed the process as much as I should have." That didn't mean I hated my job. It didn't mean I didn't like it. It didn't mean it was a chore. I loved the work, but I realized I'd robbed myself of something valuable.

About a year and a half later, I was having some success building my business, I had some clients and had worked through the 2004 election, and I said to myself, "You know what? I deserve a vacation." A mentor of mine owned a home in Nassau, Bahamas, that he offered to let me use. I didn't have to pay for anything except a plane ticket. I called my brother and one of my best friends. We flew to Nassau for five days and we just breathed.

Confirmation can be a simple moment, and the celebration can be simple, too, but both carry a great deal of importance. Don't neglect them, because they're notifying you of something very important. You made it!

CHAPTER 13

Fulfillment

We've finally reached the step that is the real reason you began this journey in the first place. You read this book to get to the place where every part of you is operating cohesively at a new level—beyond where you've ever been before. Do you remember how you felt when you first started reading this book? Were you unsure, a bit disconnected, or unclear about the place that you were going to strive to reach? All of those feelings were a byproduct of operating in a space that was less than your best.

My journey began in 2003. I was probably at the lowest point in my life—unemployed, broke, dealing with a failed marriage. I wasn't spending very much time with my children. My personal relationships were fragmented because I was coming out of a period of depression, and when I wasn't depressed, I was working hard to try to get something going.

It was at that point that it hit me. "Wait a minute. This is ridiculous. This is no way to live!"

Although I was not a senior executive at a Fortune 500 company, I'd been on the senior staff of the largest and oldest civil rights organization in the world, something I wanted and loved doing. At a very young age, I'd reached one of the places I wanted to be in my professional life, but it wasn't enough. It wasn't enough to be professionally successful. It wasn't enough to travel around the country. It wasn't enough to receive standing ovations at my speeches. It wasn't enough to have gained some small bit of celebrity.

It wasn't that it wasn't satisfying enough, but too many pieces were missing, and there was still so much more of my life, both professional and personal, that I wanted to accomplish. At that point in my development I began to shift gears, and told myself, "My life can't just be about how I'm going to build this business. It has to be about how I'm going to build my life."

Over the last six years, since coming to that realization, I've developed a much better relationship with my children. I'm still building on it, because that never stops. I still don't see them as much as I want to, because I'm still running like crazy, but the quality of the time that we spend together has dramatically improved. As I continue to increase the level of fulfillment in the relationship I have with them, I know that I've come a long way. I've also been able to create the kind of professional life that allows me to do what I love doing, without taking directions from someone else (most days), and being paid for doing it.

At the same time, I've been able to solidify a circle of friends who communicate and support each other on a level that enriches my life. There was a time when I would go weeks without talking to them, but now there's seldom a week that goes by when we don't at least e-mail or send a Facebook message. I still don't hang out with them every weekend, but we know what's going in each other's lives and are there to support each other with consistency.

Finally, my dad is currently fighting cancer, and I'm watching my mom get older, but no more than two or three days pass before I have a real conversation with both of them. It can be about what I'm doing or what they're doing, or something hilarious that my kids said or did, or their advice about something that I'm doing. Now I don't ever feel that I miss my parents, even though I don't live where they do, because we're in such close contact. They are my best friends.

I feel good about where my life is right now and excited about the fact that I've created a process that will help me maintain it and take me to the next level.

Now that you've gone through your journey from blow-up to confirmation, you, too, should feel differently about yourself and where you are. By now, you must be seeing improvements in your relationships at home, and with friends and colleagues, as well as better ways of working and following your career path, and a healthy fusion between the parts of your life that used to battle each other.

You may not have changed your whole life, but you've changed how you look at it, and your idea of what you believe you're capable of. You may have changed what you were working for and how you did it. You're not a different person, but you're living your life in a different way.

You've also realized that reaching your personal best is not about being perfect. You know you aren't going to wake up one day and discover everything about you is fabulous. You're always going to face issues, challenges, and unexpected tests, which may come from the outside as well as inside. But you now look at these challenges differently, and face them with resources that were unknown to you a year ago.

Reaching our personal best doesn't make us deities. Reaching our personal best means that we're striving for the best within us, and we're fighting as hard as we can to get out of our own way. Now you've gotten yourself to a place where you see yourself for who you are, and you can envision yourself raising the bar and putting forth the energy and effort it takes to pursue your best in every aspect of your life. The place you have arrived at fills you with a sense of wholeness and peace.

The feeling that comes with you reaching this place is called fulfillment. In this chapter, we'll look at what fulfillment is, why it's so important that you found it and, most importantly, how you keep it.

A Personal-Best Fulfillment Test

You may be asking yourself, "How do I really know that I am fulfilled?" I believe that being fulfilled means you're satisfied or happy because you fully developed your abilities or character, or realized completely your ambitions and potentialities. However, how do you know, in a really tangible way, that you've reached this place where you're actually fulfilled? After all, most of us don't cross some invisible finish line and proclaim, "Okay, now I'm fulfilled." You don't get a text message or e-mail that says, "Congratulations, you made it!" In my own case, I didn't realize I was there until I didn't feel the things that I used to feel on a regular basis.

You'll be happy to know, however, that there actually is a Personal-Best Fulfillment Test. You know I wouldn't leave you in the cold without a test. Remember the map you created back in Chapter 8? Now is the perfect moment to pull it out, look at where you were when you started, where you said you wanted to be, and consider where you are now. Remember when you went through the process of constructing your map, I didn't just ask, "Where do you want to be?" I also asked, "How will you *feel* when you get there?"

Being your personal best is not just about checking off benchmarks on a list of things that you want to accomplish. It's about how you feel when you get there, because that feeling tells you if the things you're doing and attaining are meaningful. Once you reach your personal best, you're no longer doing things just to do them. You're doing them because they add value to your life and the lives of those around you, and those things are better quantified by how you feel than what you have.

We're taught, especially men, to devalue our feelings and emotions in the name of gaining stuff. I'm not recommending that you become some overly emotional ball of sensitivity. Nor am I telling you to ignore your feelings, because they're a reflection of where you truly are.

So, what does it feel like? Look at where you started, where you said you wanted to be, and how you thought you'd feel when you got there. Now, process that. Take a moment to write, either in your Power Notes or on a paper bag, how you feel about where you are right now in the various parts of your life.

How do you feel about your family life?

How do you feel about your spouse or your significant other and the relationship you have? Don't write about the person; write about how you feel about the relationship.

How do you feel about your professional life? Not about where you're working, or what you're doing, or how much you're paid, but about how you feel when you walk into your workspace, or when you're in the process of doing your job every day. These things reflect where you are.

Now compare those feelings to the ones you had when you started this journey by looking in the rearview mirror and remembering where you were when you first started. Look not only at what you've done from the time you started this process, but also at how you've transformed, how you feel about yourself, about what you're doing, about how you're doing it, about your relationships, and your job. Can you say to yourself that where you are now is a place that is more empowered than where you started?

Do you feel satisfied about the work you do? Do you feel that your relationships are meaningful? Do you feel that the time you spend with your family is engaging and enriching?

Your answers will help you determine if you've actually reached a place of fulfillment. And if you have, are you still on your way? This is not the time to beat yourself up over how unfulfilled you are. Some of you may have hit every mark, and you should congratulate yourselves for that. Some of you may be doing great in one area, but are still working on another, which is fine because this is a process. The important question is: Are you more fulfilled than you were when you started?

If you are, you know that you're on the path to reaching your personal best.

Everybody's road to his or her personal best is different. Some of us get there quickly—perhaps in the time it takes to read this book. Others take longer, perhaps another week, another month, another year. What you can be assured of is that the process that got you from where you started to where you are is the same process that's going to get you from where you are now to where you want to go.

The second thing you need to do is look at the areas of your life that you once neglected or ignored. How do you feel about the progress that you've made in those areas? This assessment is critical because it allows you to gauge not only the changes you've made in your life, but how you actually feel about them.

Think about it. If you're working on a scale of one to ten, and you're operating at a level 7 of fulfillment in your job but you're at only at level 2 in your family life, yet you rose to 5 in your family life and 8 in your job, you've grown. And you need to celebrate that—because even though you're not yet where you want to be, you've made a great deal of progress.

When you've done all you set out to do, that is fulfillment—a place where you can do things that you couldn't and wouldn't before. That is your personal best.

A Personal-Best Maintenance Plan

Now that you got here, how can you stay here? For this feeling of satisfaction, wholeness, completion, and fulfillment to remain, you still have work to do. You can't just take it for granted, kick back and say, "Okay, I've arrived."

Reaching your personal best is not about getting to one destination, like athletes do after winning the Super Bowl. Sure, take a moment to celebrate. Then, unlike the Super Bowl MVP, who says he's going to Disney World to celebrate his achievement, you're more like Barack Obama who, after winning the election, was back to work the next day. There's always more work to do.

So take time to use your inauguration to celebrate reaching your personal best. But understand that after the inauguration—which is, after all, only one day—you have to keep pushing forward to reach the next level. The feeling of satisfaction that you have is great, but you have to maintain it. Remember, you've made it to your personal best. Now that you are here, how do you stay here?

To help you do this, I've created a Personal-Best Maintenance Process, and I recommend that you go through it once a month. If you own a car, you know that, to keep it running, you have to maintain it regularly. From an oil change to a tune-up to putting air in the tires, a responsible driver realizes that whether that car is a Ferrari or a Ford, if you want to keep it running at its best, you need to put a maintenance process in place.

You need the same care if you want to keep running at your best. It's not enough to simply get here, because if you don't keep working to stay here, then you'll have wasted your time. Your maintenance program is a monthly, 5-step process.

- Remember where you started: Never forget how far you've traveled. This not only gives you a sense of how much work you've put in to get here, but how far you'd actually fall if you stopped. Be thankful for the process and realize that if you made it this far, you can actually go farther. Frequently, it's that first step out of the 5-block radius of where you live that's the hardest. I sometimes think about people who've reached the highest peak in their industry or profession—the professional athlete, prominent politician, corporate CEO, the platinum-selling artist. Too often, they forget where they started. Or they get comfortable, perhaps because they believe their press, or because they're seduced by the money or the acclaim, and they begin to feel they've been at that pinnacle all the time. You have to remember that you haven't been here all your life. It took a lot of work to get here, and it's going to take as much work to stay here. If we forget for even a moment how far we've traveled, it can put us in a space where it will be easy to revert even further than where we started.

- Update your vision: Continue to assess where you want to be. Your personal best will evolve as you evolve. Don't be afraid to refine your vision regularly for the next stage in one or all parts of your life. Remember, they're all connected.

- Advance your strategy: Refined visions need advanced strategies. You have to know how you're going to get where you're going. Learn new methods, and put them into action to help you get from where you are now to that new place—the evolved personal best.

- Manage your team: Make sure your team can get you where you want to go as your goals change. Replacing old members with new ones does not mean that you remove people from your life or friendship circles. But some of the places you have yet to go will require that you roll with people that you have yet to meet. So keep an eye out for them.

- Remember the feeling: Never lose the feeling you have now. The whole you needs to be fed. The more you embrace feeling good about the whole you, the longer you'll be able to remain in the space of your personal best. You've given your best effort, now enjoy feeling your best. It's also important to be thankful for each step of the process you've been through.

When my friend Farrah Gray was sixteen he sold his company that marketed food to kids and became a millionaire. That wasn't even his first venture. Farrah started selling rocks in the projects—and I'm not talking about crack. These were real rocks that Farrah found and painted, selling them as paperweights or anything else his fertile imagination could conjure up to entice people to buy a rock.

He created business cards from pieces of cardboard saying "21st Century CEO," and he went around the community handing them out to everyone he saw. One day, a man asked him what his company was, and Farrah admitted he didn't know. He just knew he was a CEO. He now runs a multimillion-dollar company that does everything from venture capitalism to media, and has written several bestselling books. Farrah is only twenty-five years old, but he has come a very long way. If, for some reason, he begins to get discouraged about where he's trying to go, all he has to do is think about how far he's come. As he puts it, "If I could come from the projects of Chicago and become a millionaire before I was twenty, how much farther can I go now?"

Farrah keeps a picture in his office of himself as a kid carrying around a red lunchbox that he used as his briefcase. That picture serves as a regular reminder of just how far he has come. It's important to have a tangible reminder—whether it's a picture like Farrah's, or a note that someone gave you, or an article, or a book, or the first dollar you ever made to remind you of where you started, where you once were. That can be a great motivator.

In my home, on my desk, I keep a container of soil from Ghana, which I collected the first time I went to Africa. I collected it from right outside a slave castle in Elmina. I was a college student at the time, and it was a really pivotal point in my life, because it was then that I decided I wanted to be an activist, I wanted to be an organizer. Part of going to Africa for me was this cultural connection with who I was and where I'd come from. I thought about the people who were slaves in America who'd come from this soil, and that, if they could come to America in chains and ultimately create a thriving subculture, what excuse did I have for not using all the opportunities, abilities, and gifts I'd been given to create a great life for myself?

I've kept that soil with me ever since. In fact, I'm looking at it as I write these words. I keep it in a wooden box my great aunt gave me. She was the first person in our family to go to Africa. She was a teacher for about forty-five years, and continued to volunteer at her school until she was ninety. She took a bus two or three times a week to continue to teach those kids.

She gave me the box, which she bought when she was in East Africa. She was the person who introduced Africa to me as something more than a place of poor people, civil war, and famine, but a place with an amazing culture, ingenuity, spirit, and energy. It was, I thought, appropriate that the box she gave me hold this soil.

So for me, my tangible reminder isn't a picture or a letter. Instead, it's this message from the earth, from my past, from my people. It tells me each time I look at it, that if these people could go through all that they did, I can go through the things I have to go through.

It doesn't matter what your memento is. You don't have to go to Ghana to find your personal touchstone. You don't have to have a picture of yourself with your red lunchbox. But you do need to have some way to remind yourself of the feeling you now have. You have made it.

This is the beginning of a new life. Now you can pick up one of those other books that show you how to get rich or become famous. Now you can pick up one of those other books to show you how to find a mate in thirty days. Because now, when you read those books, you start with something they can't give you. You're now living a life that's full, whole, meaningful, and powerful. You've embraced every aspect of who you are to create a method of making each aspect powerful.

As you walk out the rest of your journey, you'll continue to build, grow, challenge yourself, and succeed. You've pushed through the personal mediocrity that imprisons many people to create a life that you can feel good about. You've challenged the status quo that many people with great personal lives have used as an excuse not to excel in their professional lives. You've stretched your old false self to become your new true self, your best self. Don't look back, keep it going, because there are greater heights for you to achieve and only your best you can take you there. Now claim it, walk in it, and live the life that you were created to live. *Your best life!*

ACKNOWLEDGMENTS

I want to thank the people that helped to make this book and so much of the life that I have lived to write it possible. I had a team that every first time author who has no idea how to write a book should have. I will never be able to properly thank LaVenia LaVelle, my business partner, for going above and beyond the call of duty to support every step of this process and ensure this book happened. My agent Uwe Stender and my publisher, Tavis Smiley and my editor, SmileyBooks president, Cheryl Woodruff, for believing in this project when I gave them reason not to; I appreciate their unwavering support. To the rest of my team that worked to provide me support throughout this process, Lamell McMorris and the Perennial team, Raoul Davis and the ASG team, Ruth Mills, Rusty Fisher, and my super executive assistant Erika Mason.

I am the member of an incredible family that has provided an environment of inspiration and support that every person should be so blessed to have. Thanks to my Mom for always being the sobering voice of honesty, challenging voice of truth, and quiet, but always present source of love. And to my Dad, whose every day of living is a greater inspiration to me. Thank you for your ability to attack every situation that has tried to destroy you with a spirit of excited optimism. You have taught me not just how to survive, but to enjoy everyday in the process. Thank you Jamon for being my brother and best friend. Your presence in my life on a daily basis gives me strength. Aunt Roz, you have inspired me to keep a level of integrity in my voice as I watch you do the same. Deneia, you have supported this process even when it was inconvenient for you. Thank you for never letting the ball drop with Madison and Myles not only through this book process, but as I attempt to walk out this call on my life. And for the example of greatness and for their never-ending support I have to thank Grace and Walter Spencer, Elizabeth Clarke, Willie Pearl Johnson, the Johnson family, the Cuffari family, and Dino and Demby Hendrix.

There are a few friends who supported me in amazing ways, not just through this book process, but also through the real life experiences reflected within the journey. Without them I would have never made it. They are and have been angels in my life. Thank you Nicole Leary, Angela Bostick, Tanika Yancy, Gary Foster, Kermit Quinn, Constance Glen, Rev.

CJ Blair, Rev. Tony Lee, Carol Hardy PhD, Marvin Dickerson, and Rev. Jamal Bryant. An extra special thanks to two men who have had my back daily for over a decade. Shaun Tucker and George Rice, God has blessed me beyond any expectation by sending you into my life. And last, but certainly not least, Jacqueline Drakeford. You are my best friend. Thank you for your support throughout this entire process. I would not have made it through without you.

The people whose lives have served as practical examples for this book, those whose stories are included in the pages as well as those whose stories are reflected in my own life. The activists, entertainers, journalists, business people, and friends who are too many to thank individually. You have inspired me and I thank you.

Finally, there is a group of amazing people and organizations that were a part of my life before there was ever a book deal. They invested in me so that I would I live the life I have and prepare me to become Everything I Am. There is also an incredible group of people I am blessed to work with today. Thank you for the opportunities, support and continued inspiration. I am, in part, because of you. Thank you Rev. James Thomas Sr. and St. Marks Presbyterian Church, Ollie and Yvonne Scott and David and Anna Smith, Mrs. Nina Roseberry (Loving), Mr. Nemicheck, Cleveland Heights High School, the late Congresswoman Stephanie Tubbs Jones, Coach Claude Holland, Kevin Coburn, Rubin Paterson, Helen Cooks, Theresa Gabriel, Bishop Edward Cook, The Baldwin family, The University of Toledo Black Student Union, The NAACP, Rev. Julius C. Hope, John Johnson, Earl Shinholster, Terrie Williams, Donna Brazille, Stephen Hill, Darius "Big Tigger" Morgan, Russell Simmons, Kevin Liles, Kweisi Mfume, Russell St. Bernard, Tommy Dortch, David Sutphen, and the BET, Live in the Den, Tom Joyner Morning Show, All for Africa, Lincoln Theatre Board families.

Special thanks to all the brothers and sisters locked down and the college students all over the country whose support keeps me honest and humbled.

ABOUT THE AUTHOR

ABOUT THE AUTHOR

The host of *The Truth with Jeff Johnson*, a hard-hitting new talk show airing on BET, and a weekly commentator on the nationally syndicated *Tom Joyner Morning Show*, **Jeff Johnson**'s interviews truly "represent" from grass-roots organizers to major world figures. Johnson is a frequent guest and commentator for national media including MSNBC's *Dayside* and *Hardball with Chris Matthews,* CNN, Fox News Channel, Huffington Post, CNN.com, The Root.com, and EbonyJet.com. Johnson won a 2008 NABJ Salute to Excellence Award for BET's "Life & Death in Darfur, Jeff Johnson Reports" series. He lives in Washington, D.C.

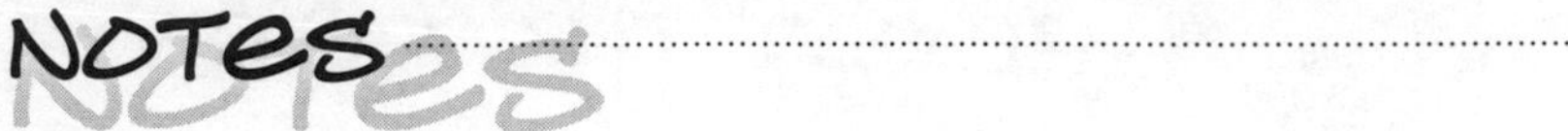

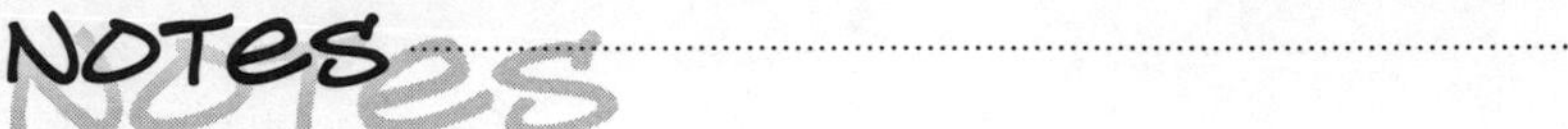

NOTES

NOTES

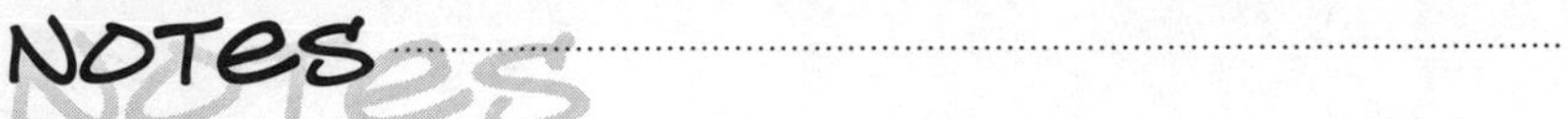

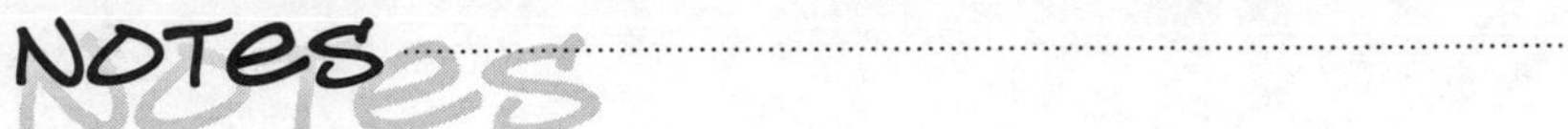

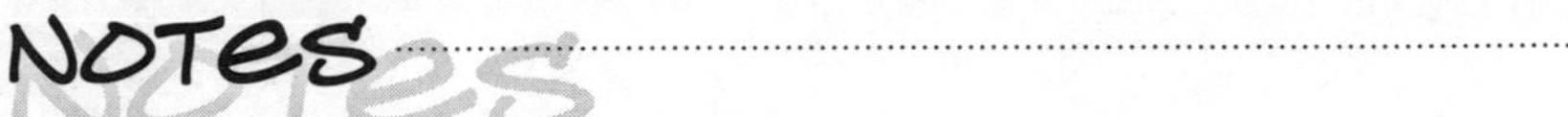
NOTES

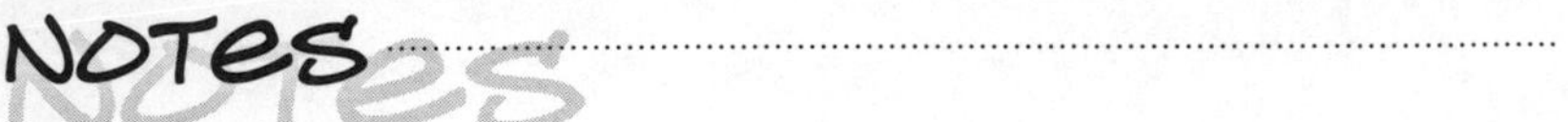

⊙ ⊙ ⊙

We hoped you enjoyed this SmileyBooks publication.
If you would like to receive additional information, please contact:

SmileyBooks

Distributed by:

Hay House, Inc.
P.O. Box 5100
Carlsbad, CA 92018-5100

(760) 431-7695 or **(800) 654-5126**
(760) 431-6948 (fax) or **(800) 650-5115 (fax)**
www.hayhouse.com® • www.hayfoundation.org

⊙ ⊙ ⊙

Published and distributed in Australia by: Hay House Australia Pty. Ltd. • 18/36 Ralph St. • Alexandria NSW 2015 • *Phone:* 612-9669-4299 • *Fax:* 612-9669-4144 • www.hayhouse.com.au

Published and distributed in the United Kingdom by: Hay House UK, Ltd. • 292B Kensal Rd., London W10 5BE • *Phone:* 44-20-8962-1230 • *Fax:* 44-20-8962-1239 • www.hayhouse.co.uk

Published and distributed in the Republic of South Africa by: Hay House SA (Pty), Ltd., P.O. Box 990, Witkoppen 2068 • *Phone/Fax:* 27-11-467-8904 • info@hayhouse.co.za • www.hayhouse.co.za

Published and Distributed in India by: Hay House Publishers India, Muskaan Complex, Plot No. 3, B-2, Vasant Kunj, New Delhi 110 070 • *Phone:* 91-11-4176-1620 • *Fax:* 91-11-4176-1630 • www.hayhouse.co.in

Distributed in Canada by: Raincoast • 9050 Shaughnessy St., Vancouver, B.C. V6P 6E5 • *Phone:* (604) 323-7100 • *Fax:* (604) 323-2600

⊙ ⊙ ⊙